SUMMER IN A JAR:
MAKING PICKLES, JAMS & MORE

Andrea Chesman

Illustrated by Loretta Trezzo

WILLIAMSON PUBLISHING
CHARLOTTE, VERMONT 05445

Library of Congress Cataloging in Publication Data

Chesman, Andrea.
  Summer in a jar.

  Includes index.
  1. Pickles. 2. Cookery (Relishes)
3. Jam. I. Title.
TX805.C44 1985 641.6'16 85-6543
ISBN 0-913589-14-4 (pbk.)

Cover and interior design: Trezzo-Braren Studio
Illustrations: Loretta Trezzo
Typography: Villanti & Sons, Printers, Inc.
Printing: Capital City Press
Cover photo: Didier Delmas

Williamson Publishing Co.
Charlotte, Vermont 05445

Manufactured in the United States of America

First Printing June 1985

Illustrated by Loretta Trezzo

Contents

Preface

Packing summer in jars — that's what I think preserving food is all about. As I fill jars with crispy cucumbers or silky, smooth peaches, I feel like I am capturing sunlight in the jars, as well as the sweet smells and pungent flavors of the freshest fruits and vegetables. Opening a jar of crunchy dill pickles or tangy grape jelly when it's cold and raw outside . . . why, it's like tasting summer all over again.

Refrigeration, freezing, long-distance trucking, and agribiz may have robbed us of the necessity of preserving our own fruits and vegetables, but nothing has replaced its rewards. Not only is there satisfaction in preserving seasonally fresh fruits and vegetables and extending the summer as long as possible, there is the satisfaction of making *healthful* preserves.

I make my own pickles and relishes because my own taste better than most commercial pickles, which are either too sweet or too salty. I also, find most jellies too sweet and I hate to think of consuming all that sugar.

Most of us are trying to cut down on the amount of salt and sugar we use in our foods. But, at the same time, we are cooking with more flavor than ever. We are cooking with more herbs and less salt to bring out the subtle, natural flavors of our foods.

The recipes in this book make jams, jellies, and preserves that taste like *fruit*. They contain surprisingly little sugar. If you want to make a jam or a jelly with equal proportions of fruit and sugar, it is easy to go to the store, buy a bottle of commercial liquid pectin, and follow the recipes that come in each package. But the funny thing about those recipes is that the final products are so sweet, most of the jams and jellies taste alike.

There are new tastes to be enjoyed in the pickle recipes. Ever tasted a Basil Bean? A pickled cucumber flavored with tarragon? A dill pickle with a touch of clove? These pickles require far less salt than most old-fashioned heritage recipes require. And less sugar, too.

You don't have to work with large quantities of fruits and vegetables to make delicious preserves and large pickles. From my garden, I get a steady stream of cucumbers, too many to eat fresh, but often too few to make into a normal-size batch of pickles. That's why I've developed a series of "Single Jar" pickle recipes. I fill as many jars as I need with cucumbers—or beans, or okra, etc. Then I measure out the salt and spices for each jar. I pour in the required amount of hot brine and finish filling with boiling water. Then I cap, seal, and process. In no time at all. And each vegetable is preserved at its peak—no waiting around in the refrigerator until I've accumulated a full batch.

I also make regular raids of my herb garden for pickle flavors. Fennel, basil, tarragon, and oregano all supplement the traditional dill. The pickles are delicious—and different.

Is pickling and preserving a time-consuming process? It doesn't have to be. I have chosen not to include old-fashioned pickle recipes that involve performing many steps over the course of several days. Where possible, I have emphasized the use of food processors, steam canners, and juice extractors to take a lot of the labor and fuss out of preserving.

No, the process need not be time-consuming. But it should be fun. Once you are hooked on the art of packing summer into jars, you will find yourself looking forward to the preserving season, as I do. Nothing beats the satisfaction that comes from seeing rows on rows of your own brightly colored canned preserves. Nothing beats the taste, either.

· 1 ·

Getting Started

The spring vegetables look great! You've savoured the first asparagus, and earliest peas. Strawberries are in abundance and soon the beans will be ready, too. The preserving season has begun.

If you have never preserved fruit and vegetables before, relax. It's easy. When you make pickles and jams and such, you are working with high-acid foods, so you have fewer worries about food spoilage than you would if you were preserving low-acid foods, like meats and unpickled vegetables. And there's no need to worry about pressure canners. A minimal investment in equipment will get you started.

Looking at Kettles, Canners, and Other Equipment

In just about every recipe, I specify using nonaluminum cookware. Aluminum and acid simply don't mix. A chemical reaction takes place when aluminum meets acid, and an off-flavor is produced in the foods.

The metallic flavor that is produced when aluminum reacts with acids isn't always discernible, so you may be tempted to use the same old aluminum cookware you've always used. But all it takes is one large batch of chili sauce to go bad (the metallic taste is most apparent in tomato and hot pepper products) to convince most people to make their preserves in nonaluminum cookware.

I use enamel-clad cast-iron cookware for all my pickling and preserving. The heaviness of the cast-iron spreads the heat evenly and prevents scorching. This is important when making jams and chutneys, which do scorch easily. I also use wooden or stainless steel spoons and utensils, as well as stainless steel sieves and strainers.

STEAM CANNERS VS. BOILING WATER BATHS

Pickles and preserves (not just fruits preserved in a jellied syrup, but jams, jellies, marmalades, and conserves, as well) should be processed in a boiling water bath or steam canner to provide a good seal and safe keeping. The only exceptions to this rule are fermented pickles, freezer pickles, and jellies. I will talk more about these exceptions later.

The most commonly used processor is a boiling water bath. This is a huge kettle that holds several quarts of water and can process up to 7 quart jars of preserves at a time. This is the piece of equipment sanctioned by the USDA for home-canning of fruits and pickles.

I use a steam canner instead of a boiling water bath, for all my processing of fruits and pickles. The steam canner has an aluminum well that holds only 2 quarts of water. Over the well is an aluminum plate, on which you put the jars you are processing. The plate has many holes to allow steam to travel up from the well and fill the dome lid with steam. The dome is the huge cover that fits over the jars and provides a space to contain the steam that processes the jars.

The steam canner has many advantages over the water bath. You only have to heat 2 quarts of water to boiling instead of the several quarts in the boiling water bath. The water can be boiling in the steam canner when you place the jars inside. The water in a boiling water bath should be hot, but not boiling, when you place the jars in. Otherwise you run the risk of breakage.

With both canners, you must wait until a good processing temperature is reached before you can start counting the processing time specified in your recipe. For the boiling water bath canner, this means waiting until the water comes to a boil, which can take close to 30 minutes.

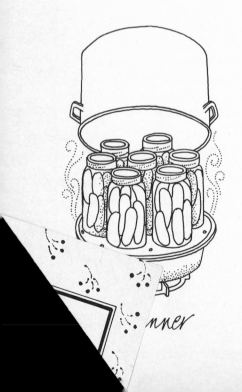

nner

If you have pickles in the canner, those pickles are going to be slowly cooking during that half hour, and that means soggy pickles. It also means a lot of waiting in the kitchen. This time really adds up when you are making more than one batch.

With the steam canner, waiting to reach a good processing temperature means waiting until you see a steady stream of steam venting from the canner for at least 5 minutes. (This may be contrary to information you received from the manufacturer of your steam canner, but it is in accordance with guidelines developed at the University of Massachusetts in Amherst.) If you preheat the water in your steam canner, it will take 10–15 minutes for the canner to reach a good processing temperature, compared to the 30 minutes with the boiling water bath. As a result, canning goes faster (and remember you didn't have to spend a lot of time preheating that water, either) and your pickles don't cook in the canner.

You don't even have to buy a new piece of equipment to fashion your own steam canner. If you have a pressure canner, you can use it as a steam canner. Place the rack in the bottom of the canner. Fill the canner with 4 inches of water. Preheat the water almost to boiling. Place your jars on the rack. Secure the lid to the pressure canner, but *leave the steam valve open* to vent steam. When you see a steady stream of steam venting from the steam release valve for 5 minutes, begin counting your processing time.

A Word of Caution: As of this writing, neither the steam canner nor the practice of adapting a pressure canner to be used as a steam canner is sanctioned by the USDA. There is no money in the USDA these days to test home-canning equipment, and they can't sanction equipment or methods they haven't tested. So home-canners are faced with a dilemma: to use these untested methods and equipment or not. This is a decision you will have to make for yourself when selecting equipment.

I've been using a steam canner to do all my fruit, tomato, and pickle processing for 4 years now. I would never want to go back to the boiling water bath. It is too time-consuming to use a boiling water

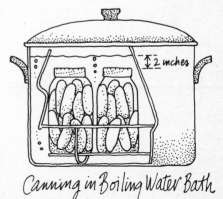

Canning in Boiling Water Bath

2-Piece Metal Lid & Screwband

← Threaded Screw Band
← Flat Metal Lid with Sealing Compound
← Rim
← Mouth
← Neck
← Shoulder

Glass Bail Wire Jar

← Glass Cap
← Rubber Ring
← Bail Wire

bath, and heating all that additional water means making an already hot job hotter. I have had no spoilage of foods with a steam canner. My pickles are crispy, my fruit firm and well-textured. In short, I have no complaints with the steam canner. All of the recipes tested for this book were processed in a steam canner, but you can use a boiling water bath if you prefer.

CANNING JARS AND LIDS

If you are just starting out, you will be buying glass canning jars that are designed to be used with 2-piece metal lids. The glass jars and the metal screwbands are designed to be reused, but the lids are not reusable. A new lid, which has the rubber seal, should be used each time you use these jars. Canning jars and lids are readily available in most supermarkets and hardware stores. Although it is hard to find the old-fashioned glass bail-wire and clamp jars, new rubber rings to use with them are still available.

FOOD PROCESSORS

Food processors save a lot of time. They slice vegetables for pickles, grate cabbage for sauerkraut, and puree fruits for jams. When a large quantity of fruit or vegetables must be finely chopped, such as when you are making a chutney or a marmalade, the food processor does the job quickly and easily. If you are planning to do any food preserving, consider using a food processor. It reduces the labor involved enough to convert a tedious chore into a pleasant culinary experience.

STEAM JUICERS

A steam juicer is another handy piece of equipment. It extracts the juice from fruits with very little mess. The alternative is to cook the fruits in a kettle and strain out the juices, using a jelly bag. While the jelly bag works fine, and it certainly is an inexpensive, low-energy piece of equipment, it's hard to avoid making a mess on your counters when you are using one. (There's more on steam juicers and jelly bags in chapter 8.)

FOOD MILLS AND STRAINERS

For a few recipes, a food mill is required to strain out skins and seeds. If you put up a lot of tomato products and apple sauce anyway, you may want to invest in a heavy-duty strainer, such as a Victorio or Squeezo.

For the recipes in this book, a simple Foley food mill, which costs less than $10 at a hardware or kitchen store, will do the job just fine.

MISCELLANEOUS UTENSILS AND EQUIPMENT

A few extra gadgets make life easier. A sharp paring knife, chopping knife, and chopping block are musts, as is a colander for draining fruits and vegetables. Sieves and strainers, a ladle, cooking spoons, slotted spoons, measuring spoons, and a grater are also handy. Don't forget that these should be made of stainless steel (or plastic), not aluminum. A minute timer will help you keep track of cooking and processing times. You probably already have many of these items in your kitchen.

A set of Pyrex measuring cups will prove to be tremendously useful. I usually ladle jellies, thin sauces, and pickling syrups and brines from the kettle into a large Pyrex measuring cup, and pour from the cup into the canning jars to prevent spills and messes.

A wide-mouth canning funnel that fits inside canning jars, well worth its low cost, helps prevent messes. A jar lifter for removing jars from the canner prevents burns and is very handy.

Finally, you will need labels for your jars. Even if the product is easily identified, you should at least date every jar. Then you can be sure that you use the oldest jars first. The labels that are packaged with canning jars work well. You can buy additional labels when your original set runs out, or you can use freezer tape. An indelible pen is a must.

THERMOMETERS

When making jellies, it is absolutely essential that you have a good food thermometer. Although there are plenty of do-it-yourself tests for determining when a jelly has gelled, none are as reliable as using a

Food Mill

thermometer. A good thermometer is a $10–15 investment, and well worth every penny.

Harvesting and Shopping Tips

Many people think of making pickles and preserves when their gardens are spilling over with fruits and vegetables, and there is more than they can eat fresh. As long as those fruits and vegetables haven't been getting wilted and dried in the refrigerator, the idea of making preserves is an excellent one. However, preserves are only as good as the raw ingredients that go into them. Less-than-perfect vegetables yield less-than-perfect pickles. And on-the-verge of fermenting and molding berries will produce quickly fermented jams, particularly when low-sugar recipes are used. So start with the best produce you can get—from your garden or your local farm stand—and use it immediately.

FRUITS

Many of us have to buy the fruit we preserve. Regardless of whether you grow your own, harvest from the wilds, harvest at "pick-your-own" farms, or buy fruit from your local farmer's market or supermarket, try to get your fruit early in the season.

For fruits such as elderberries, currants, apples, and pears, the earlier you harvest, the more pectin the fruit will contain. Pectin makes jams and jellies gel. The higher the pectin level, the better the texture your jams and jellies will have.

Also, a spot of rainy weather may cause fruits, particularly berries, to develop mold. Do not use moldy berries in preserves!

Sometimes late-harvest berries will ferment. I have had to throw out berries that I picked on the last day of the season. The berries started fermenting within hours of being picked. You can tell fermentation has begun by the smell and taste of the berries—they smell and taste like wine. If you make the berries into preserves and don't notice the fermentation, the whole batch of preserves will have an off-flavor and will go bad quickly once the jars are opened.

When you have homemade preserves, don't eat them if you suspect they have gone bad! This is true for pickles, relishes, jams, jellies, marmalades, preserves, and conserves. Throw them out where even the animals cannot get at them.

So harvest early in the season, and keep your produce cool. If you don't have space in your refrigerator, then invest in a couple of bags of ice, and store the fruit on ice in an insulated cooler, or even a clean garbage can. It is best to pick berries early in the morning before they have been heated by the sun. And it is best to preserve berries as quickly as possible. As soon as the berries are harvested, the sugars in the berries begin to be converted into starch. For best results, plan to preserve berries the day they are harvested.

Eat your less-than-perfect fruits right away. Preserve the best that you harvest for the best results.

VEGETABLES

Only perfect crispy vegetables should be made into pickles. Less-than-perfect vegetables can be made into relishes. Of course, the final results will also be less-than-perfect, but you can get away with more in relishes.

Cucumbers

Keeping cucumbers well chilled will make a big difference in how crisp your final pickles turn out. This means harvesting cucumbers in the early morning, before the cucumbers are wilted by the sun. The cucumbers should be cooled as rapidly as possible. If you can't refrigerate them immediately, try keeping them on ice. Just fill a large container or bowl with crushed ice and set the cucumbers on top.

Make pickles with your cucumbers as soon as possible. Many of the recipes in this cookbook can be made with a quart of cucumbers at a time. This means that you don't have to wait several days to accumulate a sufficient quantity to use in a recipe. Going from harvest to pickle within a day means making a crisper pickle.

This year I made my best whole dill fresh-pack (processed) pickle ever (for the recipe, see page 41). What was the secret? These pickles were made with a standard pickling variety of cucumber, but every single one was harvested when it was no longer than 3 inches. The cucumbers started out with firm, almost hard, flesh with very small seeds, and they stayed firm and crunchy.

By the way, I don't think that regular slicing cucumbers make as good a pickle as the pickling variety. The skins are tougher, and the size at maturity is too big. I grow pickling varieties exclusively, and use pickling cucumbers in salads, chilled soups, and everywhere else a fresh cucumber is called for. You can buy pickling cucumbers at the supermarket year-round, too. But supermarket cucumbers are rarely as crisp as local fresh ones are. Don't buy them if they appear dull, wilted, or shriveled.

Cabbage

Although cabbages are good keepers, the sooner you make sauerkraut or kimchee from your cabbages, the better results you will have. Stored cabbage often lacks sufficient moisture to produce enough brine from the salting process. Then you must add additional 2½ percent brine, or the sauerkraut will go bad. Remember, too, that sauerkraut can be made from red or green cabbage.

Snap Beans

As with cucumbers, you want your pickled beans to pass the crunch test. This means starting out with firm, crisp beans. Beans do not store particularly well, so harvest them when you are prepared to make pickled beans. Again, many of my recipes can be made with a quart, or even a pint, of beans at a time. So pickle your beans as they ripen, or when they appear crisp and fresh at the market.

I prefer to pickle beans when they are about 4 inches in length. After I trim off the stem end, the beans can be packed vertically in pint jars; they fit perfectly. Longer beans can be trimmed to fit, or canned in quart jars.

Harvest the beans early in the day, before the sun has had a chance to wilt them. If you don't pickle the beans immediately, keep them well chilled in the refrigerator or on ice. Refresh wilted beans in ice water before pickling.

Cauliflower

I think pickled is one of the best ways to eat cauliflower, and pickling is definitely the best way to preserve it. Frozen cauliflower becomes so mushy that it is best used in soups, but pickled cauliflower stays crispy and sharp-tasting, just like fresh cauliflower.

Cauliflower can be found in the supermarket year-round and the quality is generally quite high. It's one of the few vegetables I can recommend for pickling by the quart, year-round, as you find the time for it. Rosy Caraway Cauliflower (p. 56) makes great holiday gifts.

Since cauliflower is an excellent keeper, it can be harvested or bought and stored in the refrigerator for several days until you are ready to make pickles. Watch for brown spots, which will have to be trimmed away before you make the pickles. This won't hurt the taste of the cauliflower, but trimming away the tops of the florets does detract from its overall appearance.

If you grow your own cauliflower and you have a problem with worms, soak the cauliflower in salted ice water (¼ cup salt to 1 gallon water) for about 30 minutes. This should force the worms out of their hiding places. Be sure to rinse the cauliflower well before proceeding with any recipe.

By the way, cauliflower sometimes contains an enzyme that causes it to turn pink in the jar. The flavor is not affected, and the pickles are still good to eat.

Trimming Brown Spots on Cauliflower

Peppers

Peppers are good keepers, and they make excellent pickles. You can harvest the peppers at the desired stage of maturity — green or red (or yellow, in the case of some varieties). Shop around for special pepper varieties — sweet bell peppers can be found in green, red, yellow, and purple varieties. Peppers will keep fairly well in the refrigerator for several days, so there is no rush to make pickles immediately.

Hot peppers contain a very irritating substance, capsaicin, which is concentrated in the veins near the seeds. When handling hot peppers, avoid touching the veins and seeds with your hands, and above all, avoid touching your hands to your face. That stuff burns! It's a good idea to wear gloves when you handle a quantity of hot peppers. You may not even notice the capsaicin until it is too late. Then you will suffer a burning sensation on the affected skin for up to several hours. After handling hot peppers, be sure to wash your hands with soapy water.

Summer Squash and Zucchini

It is my opinion that you cannot make a decent pickle with an overgrown zucchini. Period. Oh, you can seed those giants, and peel them, then grate the remaining flesh to make zucchini relish. But with zucchini, as with all pickles, your pickle will only be as good as the ingredients you use. Compost overgrown zucchini! I prefer to use zucchini and summer squash that are no longer than 10 inches.

Because zucchini and summer squash are not as firm-fleshed as cucumbers, squash pickles will never be as crisp as cucumber pickles. Salting summer squash before you pickle helps in the crisping, as does making pickles as soon as you harvest. In general, I prefer cucumber pickles. However, any recipe in chapters 3 and 6 that calls for thinly sliced cucumbers can be made with thinly sliced summer squash instead.

FRESH HERBS

Although you are much more likely than ever before to find fresh herbs at your local farmstand or supermarket, I think it is well worth the small amount of effort involved to grow your own, if that is feasible. That way you always have the herbs when you are ready to make the pickles. And don't overlook the possibility of growing a few herbs in your windowbox if you don't have available garden space.

Basil and cilantro (also known as fresh coriander or Chinese parsley) can be sown in thick patches or rows as soon as the soil has warmed. They make excellent succession crops for spinach. Dill should be sown at two-week intervals throughout the season to guarantee having a supply of dill when you are ready to make pickles with beans, okra, cucumbers, summer squash, and cauliflower.

Prevent basil from flowering by continual harvesting throughout the growing season. Cut basil back to the second set of leaves.

Cilantro looks like flat Italian parsley. It goes quickly to seed if it is not continually harvested throughout the season. Harvest as you do parsley. But allow some to go to seed. Coriander seeds are wonderfully fragrant in sweet pickles.

Cilantro has a pungently sweet, smoky aroma. Some people really don't like its taste. If you don't like the smell (some people don't even like to weed near a patch of growing cilantro), you won't like its flavor in a pickle. Many people, on the other hand, adore the taste of cilantro. In the Southwest, it is commonly made into a pesto, substituting for the traditional basil.

If you buy fresh herbs, look for ones with the roots intact. To keep the herbs fresh, place them in a tall container. Cover the roots, or stems, with 2–3 inches of water. Loosely cover the leaves with a plastic bag and keep in the refrigerator. The herbs should stay fresh for 3–5 days.

When it comes to making pickles, dill is considered the queen of herbs. Sprigs of immature dill can be used interchangeably with dill heads. Or a tablespoon of dill seed can be substituted for the fresh dill,

2–3" water

Keeping Herbs Fresh

if necessary. Dill can be stored in plastic bags in the freezer for a month or so.

Garlic is used in many pickle recipes as a flavoring herb. If you use the large-bulb elephant garlic, don't cut back on the number of cloves because the flavor is so mild.

Fresh horseradish is used in many pickle recipes as a flavoring herb and as a crisping agent. Harvest the roots in the fall, before the ground freezes, or in the spring before the root sends up new shoots. You can find horseradish roots in the supermarket; it is most commonly available in early spring. One large root, bought in the spring and kept tightly wrapped in plastic in the refrigerator, will probably meet all of your pickling needs. (But don't forget about horseradish relish in chapter 4.)

To use horseradish roots, cut off as much of the root as you need. Peel away the rough skin with a sharp paring knife.

Fresh ginger root is used to flavor both pickles and preserves. It is found in the produce department of most supermarkets and in oriental food stores. Its fresh taste is much more pungent than ground ginger. When a recipe calls for a slice of ginger root, it is not necessary to peel it first.

Freeze Now, Process Later

If you are pressed for time, or can't bear the idea of standing over a kettle in the heat of the summer, you can freeze fruits first, and make them into preserves later. (You can also extract the juice now and can or freeze the juice to make into jellies later, see chapter 8.) Some vegetables can be frozen and made into relishes later.

TRAY-FREEZING BERRIES

Contrary to popular opinion, you do not need to freeze berries in sugar. Simply wash the berries, and drain well. The drier the berries are when they go into the freezer, the better their texture will be when defrosted. This is important if you are making preserves, or if some of those berries will be served in fruit salads and on pancakes during the winter. Draining on heavy towels overnight—unless its a very warm night—will produce a reasonably dry berry.

Lay the dried berries in a single layer on baking sheets and freeze. When the berries are completely frozen, remove them from the sheets and store them in plastic bags or freezer containers. I always measure the frozen berries and store them in labeled 2-cup and 4-cup batches. This way I only have to remove from the freezer as much as I need at a time.

FREEZING OTHER FRUITS

Rhubarb should be washed, sliced into 1-inch pieces, bagged, and frozen. It is as fast as that.

Plums and cherries can be washed, sliced, pitted, packed into freezer containers and frozen to be used in jams.

Peaches and apricots freeze less successfully and with more effort than these other fruits and berries. First you must go to the trouble of peeling the fruit. This is done by immersing the fruit in boiling water for about 1 minute to loosen the skins; then the skins are easily slipped off. The fruit should be halved and pitted. To prevent the fruit from darkening, it should be placed in cold water to which a tablespoon or two of lemon juice has been added. When all the fruit has been peeled and halved, drain and pack in freezer containers, toss with another tablespoon of lemon juice to prevent darkening, and freeze.

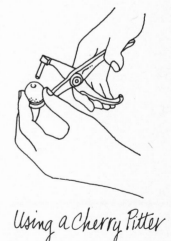

Using a Cherry Pitter

FREEZING VEGETABLES

In general, if you freeze your vegetables, your relishes will not be as crunchy as they would be if you made them with fresh vegetables. But I have been satisfied with the results of freezing green peppers and hot peppers for use in relishes later.

Peppers are tray-frozen, just as berries are. It is best to seed and chop the peppers before freezing on trays. Once the peppers are frozen, they can be stored in plastic bags. If you are planning to make sauces or relishes with the peppers, and if you have a food processor, you may prefer to seed the peppers and freeze them in halves. You can throw frozen peppers into a food processor fitted with a steel blade and chop the frozen peppers using the pulsing action.

Small cherry tomatoes can be tray-frozen, then stored in bags. Later the tomatoes can be made into sauces (and the skins and seeds strained out) or relishes.

Zucchini can be grated, salted, and drained; then frozen in bags to be used in relishes. Grate the zucchini, sprinkle with about 2 teaspoons of salt for every 6 cups of zucchini, weight with a heavy plate, and drain for at least 30 minutes. Then freeze in 2-cup or 4-cup batches in plastic freezer bags. However, relishes made with frozen zucchini will lack the crunch of relishes made with fresh, young zucchini.

ADDITIONAL INGREDIENTS

It's good to stock your pantry with some commonly used ingredients before the preserving season begins. Then you will be ready to take advantage of your harvest or seasonal shopping bargains as soon as the produce becomes available.

Sugar and Honey

Sugar and honey can be used interchangeably in recipes, although you may prefer to reduce the amount of honey when using it as a sugar substitute. However, preserves made with honey do not gel as well as those made with sugar. I usually use sugar in jellies for that reason. Also sugar makes a clearer looking jelly. Honey in a pickling brine will result in a slightly cloudy brine.

Pure maple syrup can be substituted for either of the sweeteners; it works best as a honey substitute. Remember, it does add a distinct flavor to foods. I think maple syrup is particularly nice with apple butters, as well as peach and apple jams.

Lemon Juice

Since acid activates pectin, most jelly recipes call for acid in the form of lemon juice. For convenience, I usually use bottled lemon juice, but fresh lemon juice is fine. Only a tablespoon or two is usually required. Lemon juice is not as acidic as vinegar so it cannot be substituted for vinegar in a pickling recipe. (Lemon Cukes, page 45, and Freezer Lemon Cucumbers, page 105, do take advantage of the flavor of lemons; the result is a very different and delicious pickle.)

Vinegar

As long as the vinegar has a 40–60 grain strength or contains 4–6 percent acetic acid, it can be used to make pickles. This includes commercial herb vinegars as well as homemade herb vinegars that are made from commercial strength vinegars. This is not to be confused with homemade vinegar which isn't safe, because it is untested and may not be strong enough.

White distilled vinegar is most commonly used as it does not compete with the distinctive flavors of the herbs and spices used in pickles. Rice vinegar is another relatively neutral vinegar that can be used in pickles. Cider vinegar imparts a rich, fruity flavor to pickles that is sometimes desirable, particularly in a sweet pickle.

Salt

Pickle recipes call for "pickling salt." This is regular sodium chloride, but without additives. You can substitute regular table salt for pickling salt, but you may get sediment in your jars. Pickling salt is bought in 5-pound bags from the supermarket. Because it has no additives to keep it flowing freely, it should be stored in a tightly sealed glass jar.

People who are concerned about salt in their diet can omit the salt from the brine of the fresh-pack pickles. Salt is essential in fermented salt-brined pickles, such as Half Sours, Crock Dilly Beans, and

Sauerkraut. If you must cut down on your intake of salt, skip these recipes.

Spices and Dried Herbs

Some spices are used again and again in pickle recipes. Here's a list of spices you will encounter in this book.

Allspice	*Ginger*
Bay leaves	*Mace*
Caraway seeds	*Mint*
Cayenne pepper	*Mixed pickling spices*
Celery seeds	*Mustard seeds*
Chili powder	*Nutmeg*
Cinnamon	*Oregano*
Cloves	*Pepper*
Cumin	*Rosemary*
Curry powder	*Thyme*
Dill seeds	*Turmeric*
Fennel seeds	

· 2 ·

Canning Basics

If you have never canned before, this chapter is for you. It provides a step-by-step explanation of the process of canning. The steps are basically the same whether you are making fruit preserves or pickles.

STEP 1: PREHEATING THE CANNER
AND PREPARING THE JARS

The first thing I do when I am making preserves or pickles is fill the canner with water and begin preheating. The water well of a steam canner should be completely filled. Fill a boiling water bath about half full. You will need more water to cover the jars once they are in the boiling water bath. Heat the additional water in a kettle.

To prepare jars and lids, wash the jars in warm soapy water, rinse, and drain. Anytime you process for less than 10 minutes, you must sterilize your jars before they are filled. Since most of the pickles and preserves in this book are processed for 5 minutes only, sterilizing is necessary.

To sterilize your jars, first wash them in warm, soapy water. Then immerse them in water (in the boiling water bath) and boil for 10 minutes. If you have a steam canner, place the jars upside down in the canner and steam them for 15 minutes. Leave the jars in the canner until your preserves or pickles are almost done. Then remove the jars

Preheating Water
for
Boiling Water Bath

Half Full

and drain them upside down on a clean towel on your kitchen counter. Some dishwashers have a sterilizing cycle, which can be used to sterilize canning jars. Leave the jars in the dishwasher until you are ready to use them.

Prepare the canning lids according to the manufacturer's suggestions. Usually this means washing them in warm soapy water, then rinsing the lids and covering them with boiling water. Let the lids stay in the water until you are ready to use them.

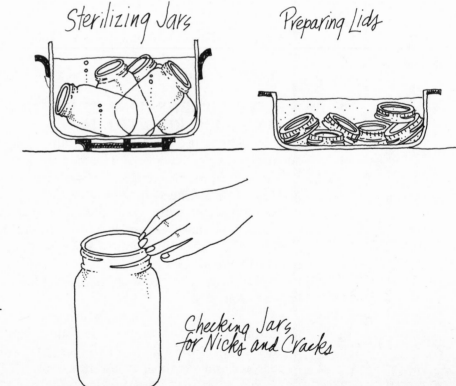

Sterilizing Jars

Preparing Lids

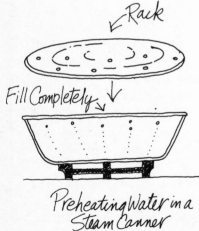

Rack

Fill Completely

Preheating Water in a
Steam Canner

Checking Jars
for Nicks and Cracks

STEP 2: PREPARING THE FRUITS
OR VEGETABLES AND BRINE

Wash your produce first to remove any surface dust or pesticide residues. A vegetable scrub brush does a good job on tough-skinned cucumbers, beets, and carrots. Scrub off the blossom end on cucumbers. Drain the washed produce. Next, just follow the recipe directions for chopping, dicing, or pureeing your fruits and vegetables.

Then follow the recipe directions for preparing the pickle brine or cooking the preserves.

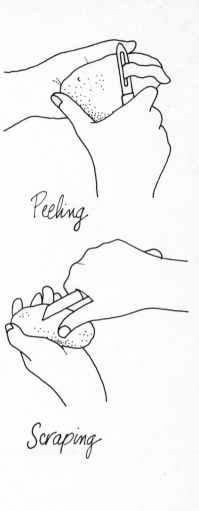

Peeling

Scraping

Scrubbing The Fruit

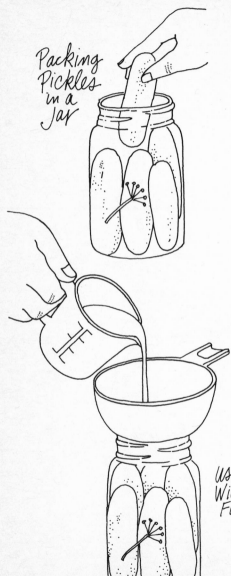

Packing Pickles in a Jar

Using a Wide-mouth Funnel

STEP 3: PACKING THE JARS

Preserves. Ladle or pour hot preserves into the jars, leaving the amount of head space required by the recipe. Head space refers to the space left between the top of the preserve and the top of the jar.

Pickles. Pack pickles into jars firmly. Try to get as much in the jar—without squashing any of the vegetables—as possible. This prevents the pickles from floating in the jar, which is unattractive. Then pour the hot brine over the pickles, leaving the proper amount of head space. The pickles should be covered by the brine.

A wide-mouth canning funnel will help you pack the jars with a minimum of spilling.

Once the jars are packed, remove any air bubbles. To remove the air bubbles, run a nonmetal spatula or chopstick around the inside of the jar. This mixes things up sufficiently to allow the bubbles to escape. If necessary, add more brine to maintain the proper head space. Do not use a metal spatula or knife because a sharp tap with a metal utensil could break the jar. Gently tap fruit butter jars against a wooden table or counter. This usually will cause the bubbles to escape. Failure to remove air bubbles may result in the jars not sealing or breaking in the canner.

Removing Air Bubbles with a Chopstick

STEP 4: SEALING THE JARS

First wipe the rims of the jars clean, with a clean damp cloth. If you are using the 2-piece metal screwbands and lids, place a lid on each jar. Screw the metal screwband into place. Hand-tighten just enough to secure everything in place. Don't use excessive force. The jars are now ready to be placed in the canner.

If you are using the bail-wire jars, place a new rubber ring on the shoulder of the jar. Put the glass lid in place. Fit the longer of the two clamps in place, leaving the other clamp up. The jars are now ready to be placed in the canner.

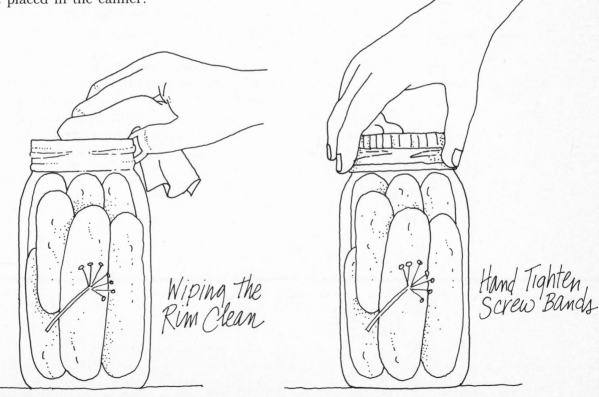

Wiping the Rim Clean

Hand Tighten Screw Bands

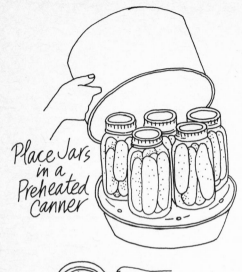

Place Jars in a Preheated Canner

STEP 5: PROCESSING

Water Bath. Place the filled jars in the preheated canner. The water in a boiling water bath should be hot, not boiling. If necessary, add boiling water from a reserve kettle so the jars are covered with a couple of inches of water. Turn the heat on high and wait for the water to come to a full boil before you start counting your processing time. The water will come to a boil faster with the lid in place.

Steam Canner. If you are using a steam canner, place the filled jars in the preheated canner and cover with the dome lid. Turn the heat on high to bring the water to a boil. Once a steady stream of steam has vented from the steam canner for 5 minutes, begin counting your processing time. Process for the amount of time specified in the recipe.

When the processing time is up, remove the jars from the canner. Now is the time to complete the seals with the bail-wire type jars. Simply pull the second clamp down. When you read in a recipe, "Adjust the seals if necessary," it refers to pulling the second clamp down on the bail-wire jars. Jars with screwbands do not need to be adjusted.

Let the jars cool undisturbed, away from drafts, for at least 12 hours.

Set Timer

Remove Jars from Canner with Lifters and Place on dry Towel

STEP 6: TESTING THE SEALS

As the jars cool, they should seal. Often you can hear the jars sealing with their familiar "pop." With Mason jars (with the 2-piece lid and screwband), you know a jar has sealed when the center of the lid is depressed. Pick up a sealed jar by its lid, and the seal will hold. With a 2-piece metal lid and screwband or with a glass bail-wire and clamp jar, if you tilt a sealed jar, it will not leak. Store any jars that have not sealed in the refrigerator and use within a few weeks.

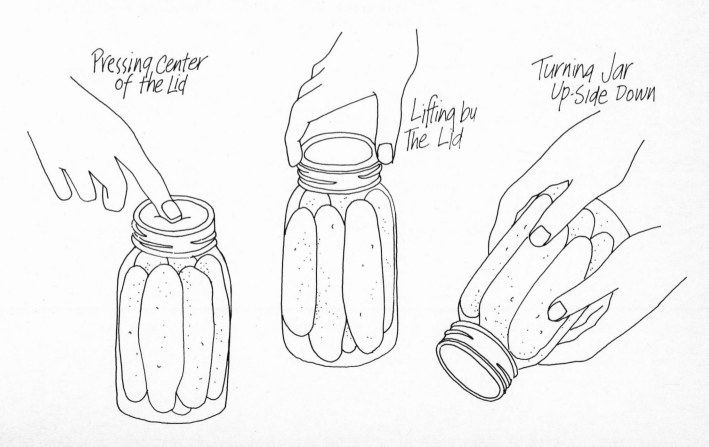

Pressing Center of the Lid

Lifting by The Lid

Turning Jar Up-Side Down

STEP 7: STORING CANNED PRESERVES AND PICKLES

Sealed jars should be stored in a cool, dry place. Remove the screwbands before storing to prevent them from rusting onto the jars. Preserves that are stored where the temperature is too warm will "weep" (beads of water will form on the surface). The storage area should be dark to prevent a loss of color. Be sure to label all your jars with the name of the recipe and the date. Most pickles should be allowed to sit unopened for at least 6 weeks to allow the flavors to develop. Use your oldest preserves and pickles first. It is best to use all of your home-canned foods within 1 year.

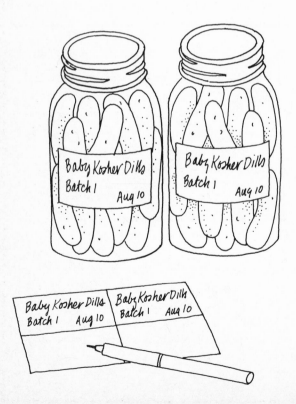

· 3 ·

Easy Single Jar Pickles

The recipes in this chapter are special. They can be made in small quantities—just a single jar at a time, if you choose. Or, if you have the time and ambition you can simply multiply the quantities and create a whole pantry of pickles. In any case, they have been specially developed to take the fuss out of making pickles.

I've never liked the idea of putting up jars and jars of the same kind of pickle. Working in large batches is tiring, especially in the heat of the summer. Also, I get bored eating the same pickles all the time.

Evidently lots of other people get tired of the same old pickles all the time, too. For a while I hosted an annual pickle-barter party—giving friends a chance to swap homemade pickles. Bread and butters were swapped for dills, and dilly beans went like hot cakes. Everyone was delighted to take home a new assortment of homemade pickles.

Then I got an even better idea: why not figure out how to make pickles a single jar at a time. Initially, my main goal was to introduce variety to the pickle shelf, but as I undertook the project, more and more advantages came to light.

By working in small quantities, you see, you can take advantage of the limited amount of surplus most gardens produce, while the vegetables are still at their peak. No more waiting around until the refrigerator bin fills with cucumbers or beans. You can make pickles whenever you have an extra quart of fresh vegetables handy. When you have just a little of this and a little of that, you can make something like Basil Jardinére, turning odds and ends into a very delicious and very showy pickle.

And the vegetables don't have to be homegrown either. With single quart jars you can take advantage of farmers market and supermarket bargains. No more calling around to local farmers and roadside stands to find out who will sell you a bushel of produce. In small quantities, you can handpick each vegetable and select only perfect ones — unlike the days of buying a case of cucumbers, only to find the ones on the bottom bruised and molding.

Working in small quantities, the process of making pickles takes very little time at all. Because I use a time-saving steam canner, pickling goes very, very fast. From start to finish, sometimes as little as 20 minutes. And only a few minutes more if I've multiplied the recipe to put up more than one jar.

Finally, experimenting with new recipes and new ideas becomes very easy. If it turns out that you don't really like a particular recipe, there are no extra jars of an unpopular pickle to haunt you — too good to throw out, not good enough to enjoy.

I think the single jar recipes in this chapter will enable you to find new recipes that will be truly pleasing. And new many of them are! By working in small quantities, I found myself freer to experiment with herbs that you don't usually find in pickles — such as basil and tarragon. And I hope you will experiment, too. Next year, I'll bet you come back to the single jar recipes with a plan to multiply the recipes to provide a supply of tasty pickles all year-round.

In addition, you'll find some excellent single jar salt-brined pickle and kraut recipes in chapter 5, as well as single jar freezer pickles (the easiest pickles of all) in chapter 6.

The Art of Making Fresh-Pack Pickles

These pickles are called "fresh-pack" pickles because they are made by packing a fresh vegetable into a canning jar, covering the vegetable with a vinegar brine, and processing in a canner. The vinegar brine is either sweetened and flavored with spices or it is made with salt and flavored with herbs and spices.

Curing with vinegar, as fresh-pack pickles are cured, is as old an art as fermenting in a salt brine. The Romans were said to be fond of vinegar pickles, and they probably picked up the technique from the Greeks or early Etruscans. The step of processing in a canner was added fairly recently. Although there isn't much in the way of bacteria or mold that can thrive in vinegar, processing destroys all the harmful bacteria and molds; it guarantees the safety of the product. Whether you are making up just 1 jar or several, you must process these pickles in a canner.

The Process of Making Fresh-Pack Pickles and Relishes

Putting up fresh-pack pickles involves careful washing and preparation of the vegetables, mixing up the brine, packing it all in jars, and processing. While there's nothing complicated about any of these steps, there are a few practices to follow to guarantee that your pickles stay crispy.

PREPARING THE VEGETABLES TO ENSURE CRISP PICKLES

The goal in making pickles is to make flavorful *crisp* pickles. That crispness is essential. Nobody likes soggy pickles. How you handle your raw vegetables has a lot to do with how crispy your pickles will be.

Slicing Thinly

MOR

SPECIAL SALT
FOR COOKING
CANNING &
PICKLES

5

Soak in iced Salt Water
To Remove Moisture

Keeping Your Vegetables Fresh

As I mentioned in chapter 1, it is very important to keep your vegetables well-chilled. Make your pickles as soon as possible after the vegetables are harvested. A vegetable that is limp when it goes into a jar will make a limp pickle.

Also, pickling cucumbers make crisper pickles than regular cucumbers. And the smaller the vegetable you harvest, the crisper the pickle. This is particularly true for cucumbers and summer squash. For whole pickles, I like to harvest cucumbers when they are 3 inches in length or less.

If you find yourself with limp vegetables, consider making relishes instead of sliced or whole pickles. Crispness is not as important in relishes—although a crunchy relish is preferred over a mushy one.

**Quick Salt-Brines for Cucumbers and
Other High-Moisture Vegetables**

Most vegetables are simply washed, sliced, and packed in a jar. But vegetables that contain a lot of moisture, such as cucumbers and summer squash, are salt-brined first. Quite simply, this means that the vegetables are tossed with salt and allowed to stand for a few hours. The salt draws liquid out of the vegetables and the result is a crisper pickle.

In most cases, I cover the vegetables and salt with cold water. This keeps the vegetables cold and distributes the salt more evenly. On very hot days, throw a tray of ice cubes into the salted water to keep the vegetables cool.

Not much salt is required for this step. Sometimes the vegetables are rinsed to eliminate excess salt before they are packed into jars; sometimes the salt is left for flavor. However, if you want to make low-salt pickles, feel free to thoroughly rinse off the salt. Keep rinsing in fresh changes of water until you can no longer taste salt when you bite into the vegetable.

Slice Thinly for Crisp Slices

How you slice your vegetable will affect its crispness quotient. Cucumbers have a crunchy skin and a softer center. The thinner you slice, the greater the proportion of crunchy skin to softer center, and the crisper your pickle will be.

I use the slicing blade on my food processor for slicing cucumbers and summer squash. I used to use the thin slice blade until I got complaints that my sliced pickles didn't have enough substance. Now I use the regular slicing blade and I find there's not that much difference in crispness. There is a *big* difference in crispness between the regular slicing blade and the thick slice blade; don't use the thick slice. There is no way that you can hand slice a cucumber as thinly or as uniformly as the food processor, unless you have practiced the technique for years and years. If you are slicing by hand, aim for slices that are uniformly ⅛ – ¼ inch thick.

Crisp Whole Pickles and Pickle Spears

Whole pickles and pickle spears are not salt-brined before they are packed into jars. What affects the crispness here more than any other factor is how firm the cucumbers are to begin with. If you really want crispy whole pickles, use tiny cucumbers. You can't go wrong with them.

Rinse to Remove Excess Salt

Bigger pickles will be reasonably crisp if you keep the cucumbers well-chilled and if you use recently harvested cucumbers.

Alum and Other Additives

Old heritage recipes call for alum as a crisping agent. There's no doubt that alum, an aluminum-based compound makes for a crisper pickle. However, there are some real questions about its safety. Dietary aluminum has been linked to premature senility and other degenerative diseases. Eating large amounts of alum can cause nausea. None of the recipes in this book use alum.

Slaked lime, or calcium hydroxide, and calcium choloride are two other compounds sometimes used as crisping agents. I just don't find them necessary.

Grape leaves, cherry leaves, and horseradish leaves and roots have long been used as crisping agents in pickles. Many people swear by them, and I have read studies proving that they contain tannins which do indeed act as crisping agents. However, one summer I made up several batches of identical pickles — except some were made with grape leaves and some without. Then I conducted a blind taste test with some friends. The results? No one could detect any difference in crispness between those pickles made with grape leaves in the jars and those made without the leaves. I still add grape leaves to my pickling crocks, but I don't bother with them for fresh-pack pickles. Add them if you like. I do add horseradish root to fresh-pack pickles. I like the tangy hot flavor it adds to pickles — whether or not it contributes to the pickles' crispness.

Steam Canners

I really do think that steam canners are a major factor in producing crisp pickles. The extra time it takes a boiling water bath to come up to a boil once the jars have been added can be the difference between a limp and a crisp pickle.

MAKING UP THE BRINE

After you have prepared the vegetables, the next step is to prepare the brine according to the recipe. Nothing complicated about that. Here are some tips that may save you some problems.

One of the reasons that I have developed single jar recipes is to enable you to pick and choose among new recipes. When trying out a new recipe, it is a good idea to make up just a jar or two. If it turns out you don't like the taste, you won't find yourself faced with a dozen more jars of an unpopular pickle. Sometimes you can adjust a recipe slightly to make it suit your tastes better.

If a brine tastes too tart, don't dilute the vinegar with water. The vinegar is needed for safe preservation. Add more sweetener instead.

If a brine doesn't taste spicy or flavorful enough, add additional spices with caution. Remember that as the jar sits, the flavors will develop.

You can substitute honey for sugar, but the brine will be slightly cloudy. Since honey is noticeably sweeter than sugar, cup for cup, reduce the amount of honey in pickles. Add enough to taste good to you.

You can substitute one type of vinegar for another, but the flavor will definitely be altered. Generally, it is better to substitute white vinegar for cider or wine vinegar than vice versa. And do remember to always use a commercial vinegar of 4–6 percent acidity.

PACKING THE JARS

Refer back to chapter 2 on how to process pickles and preserves. Most of the pickle recipes in this chapter call for processing, and most are processed in sterilized jars. I prefer to pack most of my pickles in pint jars, rather than quarts. I use quarts only for pickles that are very popular in my house—whole cucumber dills, beans, cauliflower, peppers. Also, I pack mixed vegetables and large vegetables such as whole green tomatoes in quarts because you can't fit that many in a pint. But for slices, I use pints. This way my refrigerator doesn't fill up with jars of pickles that contain only a slice or two.

When packing pickles, <u>pack spices into the jars first</u>; otherwise they will float on top of the brine. <u>Then pack the vegetables</u>. Pack the vegetables firmly. Don't squeeze the vegetables to the point of bruising them, but do pack firmly. This prevents the pickles from floating in the jar (which isn't attractive).

When packing the vegetables in the jars, leave a little more than ½ inch head space, to leave space for the brine to completely cover the vegetables. Usually brine is poured in to leave a <u>½ inch head space.</u> Leaving the proper head space is necessary for the jars to seal properly.

When you are packing cucumber slices, zucchini slices, beets, and other vegetables, you will inevitably trap some air bubbles in the jars. These bubbles must be removed or the jars may fail to seal properly. To remove the air bubbles, run a spatula or chopstick around the inside of the jar.

When Neatness Counts

A wide-mouth funnel will enable you to pack your jars with very little spillage. I usually pour my heated brine into a large Pyrex measuring cup, and pour from the cup into the jars through the funnel. This reduces spills.

SEALING AND PROCESSING

The jars are sealed and processed according to the instructions in chapter 2. After the jars have cooled, don't forget to check for seals.

If you find an unsealed jar, don't bother to reprocess. Store the jar in the refrigerator and use quickly.

Be sure to label all your jars. Store sealed jars in a cool, dry place. Allow pickles to set for at least 6 weeks before opening so the flavors will develop. Once opened, store your pickles and relishes in the refrigerator.

What About No-Salt Pickles?

Most fresh-pack cucumber pickles call for salting the cucumbers and letting them stand for 2-3 hours. This step guarantees a crisper pickle, but it is definitely not necessary. If you must make no-salt pickles, skip this preliminary step.

If a trace amount of salt is acceptable, I recommend salting the pickles, then rinsing off all traces of salt, until you can no longer detect it when you taste the vegetable.

Salt can be considered an optional ingredient in the fresh-pack pickles. It isn't needed for preserving. However, the salt adds certain depth to the flavor, even with sweet pickles. Skip the salt if you must; but remember that a little salt does round out the flavor.

WHAT WENT WRONG?
Usually what goes wrong with a batch of pickles is that you just don't like the flavor. Sometimes the pickles or the brine don't look right. Here's a listing of possible problems and causes.

PROBLEM	POSSIBLE CAUSE
Pickles are soft or slippery	Not enough vinegar Storage area too warm Water too hard
Pickles are shriveled	Cucumbers wilted from start Pickling solution too sweet Pickling solution has too much vinegar
Hollow pickles	Drought during cucumber growing season Cucumbers stood too long before processing
Dark pickles	Minerals in hard water, especially iron Use of reactive metal cookware (copper, brass, galvanized, iron) Low nitrogen levels in cucumbers
Dull or faded pickles	Poor quality cucumber — sunburned, overmature, etc.
White sediment in jar	Table salt was used
Spoiled cucumbers	Jars not sterilized Jars not sealed

• FRESH-PACK PICKLE RECIPES •

BABY KOSHER DILLS

With a recipe that can be made 1 quart at a time, there's no excuse for not picking your cucumbers when they are tiny. I like to use cucumbers for this recipe that are 2 inches long, and certainly no bigger than 3 inches.

Into each sterilized quart jar, pack 1 dill head, 1 tablespoon dill seeds, 1 teaspoon black peppercorns, 1½ teaspoons salt, 4 garlic cloves, a 1-inch piece of horseradish, and 1 quart of pickling cucumbers. Add the 1½ cups of vinegar. Fill with boiling water, leaving ½ inch head space. Seal. Process in a boiling water bath or steam canner for 5 minutes. Adjust seals if necessary. Let cool undisturbed for 12 hours. Store in a cool, dry place. Do not open for at least 6 weeks to allow the flavors to develop.

1	dill head
1	tablespoon dill seeds
1	teaspoon black peppercorns
1½	teaspoons pickling salt
4	garlic cloves
1	inch piece horseradish (optional)
1	quart tiny pickling cucumbers
1½	cups white vinegar
	Boiling water

By the Quart

QUICK DILLS

1 quart small pickling cucumbers
2 dill heads or sprigs of fresh dill or 2 tablespoons dill seeds
1 hot pepper, fresh or dried (optional)
1 garlic clove
1 bay leaf
2 teaspoons pickling salt
1 cup white vinegar
   Boiling water

By the Quart

Pack each hot sterilized quart canning jar with cucumbers. Add 2 dill heads, 1 hot pepper, 1 garlic clove, 1 bay leaf, and 2 teaspoons pickling salt to each jar. Pour 1 cup vinegar into each jar. Fill each jar to ½ inch of the top with boiling water. Seal. Process for 5 minutes in a boiling water bath or steam canner. Let cool undisturbed for 12 hours. Store in a cool, dry place. Do not open for at least 6 weeks to allow the flavors to develop.

DILL CHIPS

The mixed pickling spices give these dills a flavor that is almost sweet and very aromatic.

Combine the sliced cucumbers and salt. If you are making more than 1 pint, increase the salt up to a total of 2 tablespoons only. Toss to mix well. Add cold water to cover. Let stand for 3 hours. Then drain. Rinse if the cucumbers taste salty to you and drain again.

Combine ½ cup vinegar and ¼ cup water for each jar in a nonaluminum pot and bring to the boiling point. While the brine heats, pack the jars.

Into each hot sterilized pint jar, add 1 teaspoon dill seed, 1 garlic clove, 1 teaspoon pickling spices, and ½ teaspoon peppercorns. Fill with the cucumbers. Pour the hot brine over the cucumbers, leaving ½ inch space. Seal. Process in a boiling water bath or steam canner for 5 minutes. Let cool undisturbed for 12 hours. Store in a cool, dry place.

2 ½ cups thinly sliced cucumbers
1 ½ teaspoons pickling salt
Water to cover
½ cup white vinegar
¼ cup water
1 teaspoon dill seed
1 garlic clove
1 teaspoon mixed pickling spices
½ teaspoon black peppercorns

By the Pint

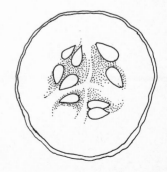

BREAD AND BUTTER PICKLES

2 ½   **cups thinly sliced cucumbers**
½   **cup thinly sliced onion**
1 ½   **teaspoons pickling salt**
      Water
½   **cup white vinegar**
3   **tablespoons sugar**
¼   **teaspoon turmeric**
1   **teaspoon mustard seeds**
½   **teaspoon mixed pickling spices**
      Dash hot pepper sauce (optional)

By the Pint

These bread and butters are less sweet than most you'll run across, which allows the flavors of the spices to come through.

In a large bowl, combine the cucumbers, onion, and salt. Mix well. If you are multiplying this recipe, do not use more than 3 tablespoons salt and be sure to rinse the cucumbers before packing jars. Cover the cucumbers with cold water and let stand for 3 hours. Drain. If the cucumbers taste salty to you, rinse and drain again.

In a nonaluminum saucepan, combine ½ cup vinegar, 3 tablespoons sugar, and ¼ teaspoon turmeric for each jar. Heat to boiling. While the brine heats, pack the jars.

Into each hot sterilized pint jar, place 1 teaspoon mustard seed, ½ teaspoon pickling spices, and a dash of hot sauce. Pack with the cucumbers and onions, leaving ½ inch head space. Seal. Process in a boiling water bath or steam canner for 5 minutes. Adjust seals if necessary. Cool undisturbed for 12 hours. Store in a cool, dry place.

LEMON CUKES

The lemon juice in these pickles gives them an unusual fruity tartness, quite different from traditional vinegar pickles—and very delicious.

In a large bowl, combine the cucumbers and peppers. Sprinkle with the pickling salt and toss well to mix. If you are multiplying this recipe, do not use more than 3 tablespoons salt and rinse the cucumbers well before packing in jars. Cover with cold water and let stand for 3 hours.

In a nonaluminum saucepan, combine 3 tablespoons lemon juice, 3 tablespoons vinegar, 3 tablespoons water, and 2 tablespoons sugar for each pint jar. Heat to boiling. While the brine heats, drain the cucumbers.

Into each hot sterilized jar, place 1 lemon slice and ¼ teaspoon allspice. Pack with the cucumbers and peppers, leaving ½ inch head space. Pour in the hot brine, leaving ½ inch head space. Seal. Process in a boiling water bath or steam canner for 5 minutes. Adjust seals if necessary. Cool undisturbed for 12 hours. Store in a cool, dry place.

2 ½ cups thinly sliced cucumbers
½ cup sliced red or green peppers
1 ½ teaspoons pickling salt
Water
3 tablespoons lemon juice
3 tablespoons white vinegar
3 tablespoons water
2 tablespoons sugar

1 lemon slice
¼ teaspoon whole allspice

By the Pint

FRESH CORIANDER PICKLES

3   cups thinly sliced
    cucumbers
1½ teaspoons pickling salt
    Water
⅔   cup white vinegar
⅓   cup water
1   garlic clove
1   tablespoon chopped fresh
    coriander
1   teaspoon black
    peppercorns

By the Pint

Coriander

Fresh coriander, known as cilantro in Mexican cookery and Chinese parsley in oriental cookery, is a very aromatic, almost perfume-like, herb. It's not a flavor everyone enjoys; but if you like the taste of the fresh herb, you'll like these pickles.

Fresh coriander is very easy to grow from seed. If you don't want to grow your own, you can purchase it from any food stores that sell Mexican or Chinese foods. Dried coriander cannot be substituted; nor can you substitute dried cilantro.

In a large bowl, combine the cucumbers and pickling salt. Toss well to coat. If you are multiplying this recipe, do not use more than 3 tablespoons salt, and rinse the cucumbers before packing in the jar. Cover the cucumbers with cold water and let stand for 3 hours.

In a nonaluminum saucepan, combine ⅔ cup vinegar and ⅓ cup water for each pint of pickles. Heat to boiling. While the brine heats, drain the cucumbers.

Into each hot sterilized pint jar, place 1 garlic clove, 1 tablespoon chopped fresh coriander, and 1 teaspoon peppercorns. Pack with the cucumbers, leaving ½ inch head space. Pour the hot brine over the cucumbers, leaving ½ inch head space. Remove any air bubbles. Seal. Process in a boiling water bath or steam canner for 5 minutes. Adjust seals if necessary. Cool undisturbed for 12 hours. Store in a cool, dry place.

DILLY BEANS

These take very little time to make. And you can make them in as big or as small a batch as your harvest requires. An opened jar of dilly beans disappears amazingly fast. They make a great snack—right out of the jar.

Trim the beans to fit into the pint jars, about 4 inches long.

In a nonaluminum saucepan, combine the vinegar and water and heat to boiling. While the brine heats, pack each clean, hot jar with 1 garlic clove, 1 onion, 1 dill head, 1 bay leaf, and 1 teaspoon pickling salt. Pack in the beans, leaving ½ inch head space. Pour the hot brine over the beans, leaving ½ inch head space. Seal. Process for 10 minutes in a boiling water bath or steam canner. Cool undisturbed for 12 hours. Store in a cool, dry place. Do not open the jars for 6 weeks to allow the flavors to develop.

2   cups greens beans, trimmed
1   cup white vinegar
½   cup water
1   garlic clove
1   small white boiling onion
1   dill head or 1 sprig of dill
1   bay leaf
1   teaspoon pickling salt

By the Pint

CHILI DILLY BEANS

2   cups green beans, trimmed
1   cup white vinegar
½   cup water
½   teaspoon pickling salt
1   garlic clove
1   dill head or sprig fresh dill
1   fresh hot pepper or 1½ teaspoons crushed red pepper flakes

By the Pint

Trim the beans to fit into the pint jars, about 4 inches long.

For each pint, combine 1 cup vinegar with ½ cup water. Heat to boiling.

While the brine heats, place ½ teaspoon pickling salt, 1 garlic clove, 1 dill head, and 1 hot pepper into each clean hot pint jar. Pack with the beans, leaving ½ inch head space. Pour the hot brine over the beans, leaving ½ inch head space. Seal. Process in a boiling water bath or steam canner for 10 minutes. Adjust seals if necessary. Cool undisturbed for 12 hours. Store in a cool, dry place. Do not open for about 6 weeks to allow the flavors to develop.

BASIL BEANS

Trim off the ends of the beans.

For each quart of beans, combine 1¾ cups vinegar and 1 cup water in a nonaluminum saucepan and heat to boiling.

Pack 1 teaspoon pickling salt, 2 garlic cloves, and 10 fresh basil leaves into each clean hot canning jar. Pack in the beans, leaving ½ inch head space. As you pack the beans, keep shaking the jar. This helps you pack evenly.

Pour the hot brine over the beans, leaving ½ inch head space. Seal. Process in a boiling water bath or steam canner for 10 minutes. Adjust the seals, if necessary. Let cool undisturbed for 12 hours. Store in a cool, dry place. Do not open for 6 weeks to allow the flavors to develop.

4	cups green beans
1¾	cups white vinegar
1	cup water
1	teaspoon pickling salt
2	garlic cloves
10	fresh basil leaves

By the Quart

ITALIAN SALAD BEANS

4 cups green beans
1¾ cups white vinegar
¾ cup water
2 garlic cloves
1 tablespoon fresh oregano leaves or 1 teaspoon dried
1 bay leaf
¼ teaspoon fresh or dried rosemary
1 teaspoon pickling salt
1½ teaspoons sugar
1 mild dried hot pepper (optional)
  About ¼ cup olive oil

By the Quart

These taste wonderful! The olive oil and fresh herbs make this an unusually flavorful pickle. Serve them on an antipasto plate as a special treat—or serve them as a pickle anytime. Don't serve the pickles directly out of the jar, however, since the olive oil will deposit a film on each bean as it is pulled from the jar. Drain off the brine and serve the beans from a glass pickle dish.

Trim off the ends of the beans.

In a nonaluminum saucepan, heat the vinegar and water. While the brine heats, pack each clean hot quart jar with 2 garlic cloves, 1 tablespoon oregano, 1 bay leaf, ¼ teaspoon rosemary, 1 teaspoon pickling salt, 1½ teaspoons sugar, and 1 hot pepper. Pack in the beans. Shake the jar as you pack to settle the beans and create space for more. Leave about ½ inch head space.

Pour the hot brine over the beans. Then fill to the top with the olive oil, leaving ½ inch head space. Seal. Process in a boiling water bath or steam canner for 10 minutes. Adjust seals if necessary. Let cool undisturbed for 12 hours. Store in a cool, dry place. Do not open for 6 weeks to allow the flavors to develop.

FRESH CORIANDER BEANS

Fresh coriander, also known as cilantro, also known as Chinese parsley, gives a delicate flavor to the beans—a change of pace from dill. The hot pepper is optional, but highly recommended.

Trim the beans to fit into the pint jars, about 4 inches long.

For each pint, combine 1 cup rice vinegar and ½ cup water. Heat to boiling.

While the brine heats, place 1 teaspoon pickling salt, 1 tablespoon fresh coriander, and 1 hot pepper into each clean hot pint jar. Pack with the beans, leaving ½ inch head space. Pour in the hot brine, leaving ½ inch head space. Seal. Process in a boiling water bath or steam canner for 10 minutes. Adjust the seals if necessary. Cool undisturbed for 12 hours. Store in a cool, dry place. Do not open the jars for about 6 weeks to allow the flavors to develop.

2   cups green beans
1   cup rice vinegar or white wine vinegar
½   cup water
1   teaspoon pickling salt
1   tablespoon fresh chopped coriander
1   fresh hot pepper (optional)

By the Pint

TARRAGON BEANS

4 cups green beans
1½ cups cider vinegar
1¼ cups water
1 teaspoon pickling salt
2 garlic cloves
3 sprigs fresh tarragon or
  1 teaspoon dried
1 teaspoon celery seeds

By the Quart

Trim off the ends of the beans.

For each quart of beans, combine 1½ cups cider vinegar and 1¼ cups water in a nonaluminum saucepan and heat.

Into each clean, hot quart jar, pack 1 teaspoon pickling salt, 2 garlic cloves, 3 sprigs fresh tarragon, and 1 teaspoon celery seeds. Fill with the beans, leaving ½ inch head space. As you pack the beans, keep shaking the jar. This helps you pack evenly.

Pour the hot brine over the beans, leaving ½ inch head space. Seal. Process in a boiling water bath or steam canner for 10 minutes. Adjust seals if necessary. Let cool undisturbed for 12 hours. Store in a cool, dry place. Do not open for at least 6 weeks to allow the flavors to develop.

CARAWAY PICKLED BEETS

Since I rarely harvest uniform-size beets for pickling, I slice them. If you have baby beets, you can pickle them whole; but you will have to make half again as much brine for each jar. You can pack more sliced beets than whole beets into a jar.

Scrub the beets well. Remove the greens, leaving about 2 inches of stem. Do not trim off the long tap root in order to prevent excess bleeding. Cook the beets in boiling water to cover until the beets test tender to the fork. This will take 20–40 minutes, depending on the size of the beets.

Cool the beets, slip off the skins, then slice or dice them. Combine the beets with the onion, caraway seeds, and salt.

For each quart of beets, heat together 1 cup vinegar, ½ cup water, and ½ cup sugar. While the brine heats, pack the beets into a clean, hot quart jar, leaving about ½ inch head space. Pour the hot brine over the beets, leaving ½ inch head space. Seal. Process in a boiling water bath or steam canner for 10 minutes. Adjust seals if necessary. Let cool undisturbed for 12 hours. Store in a cool, dry place. Do not open for 6 weeks to allow the flavor to develop.

1 quart beets (about 2 pounds)

1 small onion, thinly sliced

1 tablespoon caraway seeds

½ teaspoon pickling salt (optional)

1 cup white vinegar

½ cup water

½ cup sugar or ¼ cup honey

By the Quart

DILLED CAULIFLOWER

1⅓ cups white vinegar
1⅓ cups water
1 sprig dill or 1 dill head or 1 tablespoon dill seeds
1 garlic clove
½ teaspoon mixed pickling spices
2 teaspoons pickling salt
4 cups cauliflower florets

By the Quart

For years, I blanched cauliflower before I pickled it. One day I decided to try pickling cauliflower without blanching it first. The result: better texture and whiter color. The only drawback was that unblanched cauliflower has that characteristic "bite" to the flavor. If you prefer, blanch the cauliflower by immersing in boiling water to cover for 1 minute only, then plunge into cold water to stop the cooking action. Proceed with the recipe.

For each quart of cauliflower, heat 1⅓ cups white vinegar and 1⅓ cups water to boiling. While the brine heats, pack each hot, clean jar with 1 sprig dill, 1 garlic clove, ½ teaspoon pickling spices, and 2 teaspoons pickling salt. Pack with the cauliflower.

Pour the hot brine over the cauliflower, leaving ½ inch head space. Seal. Process in a boiling water bath or steam canner for 10 minutes. Adjust seals if necessary. Cool undisturbed for 12 hours. Store in a cool, dry place. Do not open for at least 6 weeks to allow the flavors to develop. The cauliflower may turn pink in the jar from a harmless chemical change, but it will still be fine to eat.

BASIL CAULIFLOWER

Don't be alarmed if the cauliflower turns pink in the jar. It's a harmless chemical change that sometimes occurs.

For each quart of cauliflower, heat 1⅓ cups white vinegar and 1⅓ cups water. Into each clean, hot quart jar, pack 1 sprig basil, 1 garlic clove, 1 teaspoon black peppercorns, and 2 teaspoons pickling salt. Pack with the cauliflower, leaving about ½ inch head space. Pour the hot brine over the cauliflower, leaving ½ inch head space. Seal. Process in a boiling water bath or steam canner for 10 minutes. Adjust seals if necessary. Let cool undisturbed for 12 hours. Store in a cool, dry place. Do not open for 6 weeks to allow the flavors to develop.

1⅓   **cups white vinegar**
1⅓   **cups water**
1   **sprig basil**
1   **garlic clove**
1   **teaspoon black peppercorns**
2   **teaspoons pickling salt**
4   **cups cauliflower florets**

By the Quart

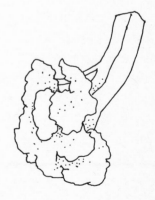

ROSY CARAWAY CAULIFLOWER

1   medium-size uncooked beet
1⅓ cups white vinegar
1⅓ cups water
1   teaspoon caraway seeds
½   teaspoon celery seeds
2   teaspoons pickling salt
4   cups cauliflower florets

By the Quart

Beets give this pickle its unusual color; caraway gives it its unusual flavor.

When making cauliflower pickles, figure that 1 medium-size head will make 2–3 quarts of pickles.

Peel the beet and chop. You should have ¼ – ½ cup. Combine the beet with the vinegar and water in a nonaluminum saucepan. Bring almost to a boil and simmer for 5 minutes.

While the brine heats, pack each quart jar with 1 teaspoon caraway seeds, ½ teaspoon celery seeds, and 2 teaspoons pickling salt. Pack in the cauliflower florets, leaving ½ inch head space.

Strain the brine and discard the beets. Pour the hot brine over the cauliflower, leaving ½ inch head space. Seal. Process in a boiling water bath or steam canner for 10 minutes. Adjust seals if necessary. Let cool undisturbed for 12 hours. Store in a cool, dry place. Do not open for at least 6 weeks to allow the flavors to develop.

DILLED JERUSALEM ARTICHOKES

Harvest Jerusalem artichokes in the late fall, after a good frost, or in the early spring. They are crisp and sweet.

Scrub or peel the Jerusalem artichokes and cut into ¼ inch slices. Combine them with the pickling salt and cover with water. Add 2 tablespoons vinegar to the water to prevent the Jerusalem artichokes from darkening. Let stand overnight. Then drain.

For each pint of Jerusalem artichokes, heat 1 cup vinegar and ½ cup water. While the brine heats, pack each pint jar with 2 tablespoons dill seeds, 1 garlic clove, and 1 teaspoon pickling spices. Pack each clean, hot pint jar with the Jerusalem artichokes, leaving ½ inch head space. Pour the hot brine over the Jerusalem artichokes, leaving ½ inch head space. Seal. Process in a boiling water bath or steam canner for 10 minutes. Adjust seals if necessary. Let cool undisturbed for 12 hours. Store in a cool, dry place. Do not open for at least 6 weeks to allow the flavors to develop.

2	cups Jerusalem artichokes
2	tablespoons pickling salt
	Water to cover
2	tablespoons white vinegar
1	cup white vinegar
½	cup water
2	tablespoons dill seeds
1	garlic clove
1	teaspoon mixed pickling spices

By the Pint

SPICY DILLED OKRA

2   cups okra pods
½   cup white vinegar
1   small dried red pepper
1   dill head or 1 sprig fresh dill
½   teaspoon pickling salt
½   teaspoon celery seeds

By the Pint

Okra pickles: you either love them or you hate them — depending on what you think of okra to begin with. I think okra pickles taste wonderfully green and, well, rather like okra.

Wash the okra. Trim off the stems, but do not cut into the okra pods.

Heat ½ cup vinegar for each pint of okra. While the vinegar heats, pack each clean, hot canning jar with 1 red pepper, 1 dill head, ½ teaspoon pickling salt, and ½ teaspoon celery seeds. Pack in the okra pods, leaving ½ inch head space. Pour in the hot vinegar, leaving ½ inch head space. Seal. Process in a boiling water bath or steam canner for 10 minutes. Adjust seals if necessary. Cool undisturbed for 12 hours. Store in a cool, dry place. Do not open for at least 6 weeks to allow the flavors to develop.

SWEET PICKLED OKRA

2   cups okra pods
½   cup cider vinegar
2   tablespoons brown sugar
½   teaspoon mixed pickling spices
½   teaspoon pickling salt

By the Pint

Wash the okra. Trim off the stems, but do not cut into the pods.

For each pint of okra, heat ½ cup cider vinegar, 2 tablespoons brown sugar, ½ teaspoon pickling spices, and ½ teaspoon pickling salt. While the brine heats, pack the okra into clean, hot pint jars. Pour the hot brine over the okra, leaving ½ inch head space. Seal. Process in a boiling water bath or steam canner for 10 minutes. Adjust seals if necessary. Let cool undisturbed for 12 hours. Store in a cool, dry place.

PICKLED PEARS

Choose a slightly underripe, firm-fleshed pear for this recipe. Seckel and Kieffer are good choices. Drain off the syrup before serving.

While you prepare the brine, hold the pears in water to cover to which 2 tablespoons lemon juice have been added.

In a nonaluminum saucepan, combine 1 cup vinegar, ½ cup water, and ½ cup honey for each quart of pears. Bring to a boil. Stick 1 whole clove in each pear quarter and pack into clean quart jars, along with 1 cinnamon stick per quart. Pour the hot syrup over the pears, leaving ½ inch head space. Seal. Process in a boiling water bath or steam canner for 20 minutes. Adjust seals if necesary. Let cool undisturbed for 12 hours. Store in a cool, dry place. Do not open for at least 6 weeks to allow the flavors to develop.

1	quart pears, peeled and quartered
	Water to cover
2	tablespoons lemon juice
1	cup cider vinegar
½	cup water
½	cup honey
	Approximately 1 tablespoon whole cloves
1	cinnamon stick

By the Quart

MIXED PICKLED PEPPERS

1 teaspoon pickling salt

1 tablespoon sugar

4 cups mixed peppers (sweet red, yellow, and green peppers, plus a few hot peppers), seeded and sliced in halves or quarters

1 ¼ cups white vinegar

About 1 cup boiling water

By the Quart

My favorite way to serve these pickles? On top of crackers and cheese, julienne-sliced and added to salads, right out of the jar.

If you don't grow a variety of red and yellow peppers, as well as the familiar sweet green peppers, look for them at the supermarket at the end of August. The mix of colors, and the slight variation in tastes, adds a great deal to these pickles. I like to throw in a couple of hot peppers — they add their fiery flavor to the whole jar. Of course, you could use this recipe with a single variety of pepper — but it won't be quite as wonderful.

Into each sterilized quart jar, add 1 teaspoon pickling salt and 1 tablespoon sugar. Pack the peppers tightly into the jar. For the best effect, pack the peppers so that the outer skins of the peppers face out of the jar. Pour in the vinegar. Fill to within ½ inch of the top with boiling water. Seal.

Process in a boiling water bath or steam canner for 5 minutes. Adjust seals if necessary. Let cool undisturbed for 12 hours. Store in a cool, dry place.

PICKLED WHOLE HOT PEPPERS

This is the fastest way I know to preserve hot peppers. In most cases, these peppers are too hot to be eaten out of hand. Sliced thinly, they can be added to a variety of dishes or sprinkled on top of nachos.

Cut a tiny slit in each jalapeño. Pack the jalapeños into hot, sterilized quart jars. For each quart, heat 2¾ cups white vinegar almost to boiling. Pour the hot vinegar over the peppers. Cap by covering with a 2-piece metal canning lid. Do not tighten the screw band.

Let the peppers stand for 1–2 weeks at a constant temperature of about 65° F.

After 1–2 weeks, the peppers should be pickled. Pour off the vinegar. Add fresh vinegar to fill each jar about three-quarters full. Add the salt and top with the olive oil. Seal. If desired, process in a boiling water bath or steam canner for 5 minutes. It is not necessary to process the peppers, however. The pickles should stay good on the shelf for several months.

1   quart whole jalapeños or similar fresh hot peppers
2¾ cups white vinegar
½   teaspoon pickling salt (optional)
    About ¼ cup olive oil
    Vinegar

By the Quart

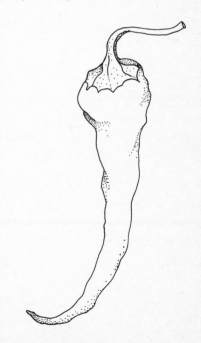

PICKLED HOT PEPPER STRIPS

1   cup white vinegar
½   cup water
1   garlic clove
½   teaspoon mustard seeds
½   teaspoon pickling salt
2   cups hot peppers, seeded and cut in strips

By the Pint

A little hot pepper goes a long way, particularly jalapeños, so I put these up in pint jars. You could even use half-pint jars. Hot pepper strips are not as hot as whole peppers, because you remove the seeds and veins before you slice the peppers into strips. Nor are they quite as firm as the Pickled Whole Hot Peppers.

Use hot pepper strips as a garnish, or substitute them for fresh hot peppers in nachos, sauces, and other cooked dishes.

In a nonaluminum saucepan, heat 1 cup white vinegar and ½ cup water for each pint of peppers.

Into each hot, sterilized pint jar, place 1 garlic clove, ½ teaspoon mustard seeds, ½ teaspoon pickling salt, and 2 cups hot pepper strips, leaving about ½ inch head space. Fill with the hot brine, leaving ½ inch head space. Be sure to remove any air bubbles that are trapped inside the jar. Seal. Process in a boiling water bath or steam canner for 5 minutes. Adjust seals if necessary. Let cool undisturbed for 12 hours. Store in a cool, dry place.

DILLED GREEN TOMATOES

Some people prefer the crock dilled green tomatoes for their crisper texture and sharper flavor; others prefer these dilled tomatoes. Either way, they take very little time to make. You can make them with any variety—just pick the tomatoes when they are small.

Into each sterilized quart jar, pack 1 quart green tomatoes, 2 garlic cloves, 1 whole hot pepper, 1 carrot stick, 1 teaspoon pickling salt, and 2 teaspoons dill. Pour in 1 cup vinegar. Fill with boiling water, leaving ¼ inch head space. Seal. Process in a boiling water bath or steam canner for 5 minutes. Adjust seals if necessary. Let cool undisturbed for 12 hours. Store in a cool, dry place. Do not open for at least 6 weeks to allow the flavors to develop.

1   **quart small whole green tomatoes**
2   **garlic cloves**
1   **hot pepper (optional)**
1   **carrot stick**
1   **teaspoon pickling salt**
2   **teaspoons dill seeds**
1   **cup white vinegar**
    Boiling water

By the Quart

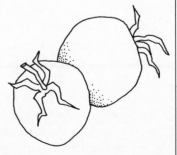

BASIL JARDINÈRE

1¾ cups white vinegar

1 cup water

1 teaspoon pickling salt

2 tablespoons fresh basil leaves

1 quart mixed vegetables (cauliflower, green beans, green tomatoes, sweet green peppers, sweet red peppers, onions, carrots, okra)

1 sprig fresh basil or 1 tablespoon fresh basil leaves

By the Quart

These layered pickles look beautiful in the jars and they taste just as wonderful. Choose your vegetables with an eye to color and take time to pack the jar carefully. The Basil Jardinère and the Tarragon Jardinère both make excellent gifts.

In a nonaluminum saucepan, combine the vinegar, water, and pickling salt. Bring to a boil. Remove from the heat and stir in the 2 tablespoons basil leaves. Cover and let the mixture steep overnight.

To pack the jars, uniformly slice the vegetables. Cauliflower should be broken into florets. Green beans should be trimmed to be about 3 inches long; all the ends should be cut at the same angle. Carrots should be sliced on the diagonal. Small green tomatoes, white boiling onions, and okra can be left whole. Cut peppers in ½ inch strips.

Place 1 sprig of fresh basil in the bottom of each quart jar. Carefully pack the vegetables in layers. Plan to have 5 to 6 layers of vegetables. An attractive arrangement begins with carrots, followed by green beans, cauliflower, red pepper, green beans, and carrots. Any colorful arrangement is fine, however. A chopstick will help you arrange and hold the vegetables in their proper positions as you pack. Try to keep the most attractive part of the vegetable facing out—the florets of the cauliflower, the skins of the peppers. Leave about ½ inch head space.

Reheat the vinegar solution almost to boiling; do not boil. Pour over the vegetables, leaving ½ inch head space. Seal. Process in a boiling water bath or steam canner for 10 minutes. Adjust seals if necessary. Let cool undisturbed for 12 hours. Store in a cool, dry place. Do not open for at least 6 weeks to allow the flavors to develop.

TARRAGON JARDINÈRE

As with the Basil Jardinère, take the time to pack the jar carefully. These pickles should look so good, you'll be reluctant to open them. Fortunately, they taste as good as they look!

In a nonaluminum saucepan, combine the vinegar, water, and pickling salt. Bring to a boil. Remove from the heat and stir in the 2 tablespoons tarragon leaves. Cover and let the mixture steep overnight to allow the tarragon flavor to develop.

To pack the jars, uniformly slice the vegetables. Cauliflower should be broken into small florets. Green beans should be trimmed to be about 3 inches long; all the ends should be cut at the same angle. Carrots should be sliced on the diagonal. Small green tomatoes, white boiling onions, and okra should be left whole. Peppers should be cut in ½ inch strips.

Place 1 sprig of fresh tarragon in the bottom of each quart jar. Carefully pack the vegetables in layers. Plan to have 5–6 layers of vegetables. A chopstick will help you arrange and hold the vegetables in their proper places as you pack. Try to keep the most attractive part of the vegetable facing out — the florets of the cauliflower, the skins of the peppers. Leave about ½ inch head space.

Reheat the vinegar solution almost to boiling; do not boil. Pour over the vegetables, leaving ½ inch head space. Seal. Process in a boiling water bath or steam canner for 10 minutes. Adjust seals if necessary. Let cool undisturbed for 12 hours. Store in a cool, dry place. Do not open for at least 6 weeks to allow the flavors to develop.

1 ¾	cups white vinegar
1	cup water
1	teaspoon pickling salt
2	tablespoons fresh tarragon leaves
1	quart mixed vegetables (cauliflower, green beans, green tomatoes, sweet green peppers, sweet red peppers, onions, carrots, okra)
1	sprig fresh tarragon or 1 tablespoon fresh tarragon leaves

By the Quart

SWEET MIXED PICKLES

1 quart mixed vegetables
(beans, carrots,
cauliflower, peppers,
onions are recommended)

1½ cups cider vinegar

½ cup sugar

¾ cup water

¼ teaspoon turmeric

¼ teaspoon mace

¼ teaspoon crushed red
pepper

½ teaspoon mustard seeds

½ teaspoon pickling salt

1 tablespoon cornstarch

¼ cup water

By the Quart

Here's a recipe designed to take care of those odds and ends of vegetables left from other pickling sessions — or just what your garden may produce some day. Don't worry about proportions of this vegetable and that vegetable. Each time you make it, it will taste slightly different — and delicious.

Prepare the vegetables. Beans should be trimmed and sliced; carrots, onions, and peppers sliced; cauliflower broken into bite-size florets. Measure your vegetables.

For each quart of vegetables, combine in a nonaluminum saucepan 1½ cups cider vinegar, ½ cup sugar, ¾ cup water, ¼ teaspoon turmeric, ¼ teaspoon mace, ¼ teaspoon crushed red pepper, ½ teaspoon mustard seeds, and ½ teaspoon pickling salt. Bring to a boil. Dissolve 1 tablespoon cornstarch in the remaining ¼ cup water. Stir into the boiling brine. Allow the brine to come to a boil.

Into each clean, hot quart jar, pack the vegetables, leaving about ½ inch head space. Cover with the hot brine, leaving ½ inch head space. Remove any air bubbles. Seal. Process in a boiling water bath or steam canner for 10 minutes. Adjust seals if necessary. Let cool undisturbed for 12 hours. Store in a cool, dry place.

The brine may settle a bit as the jar stands. Shake the jar before serving. Do not open for at least 6 weeks to allow the flavors to develop.

· 4 ·

Relishes & Chutneys

Relishes and chutneys have so many uses, I can't make enough of them. Each summer, I put up many, many jars — only to find that the crisp pickle relishes disappear on sandwiches in no time, and the sweet and sour chutneys are all given away by New Years.

The chutneys, in particular, make wonderful gifts — because they are so special and unusual. Chutneys are traditionally served as a condiment with curry dishes, but their use shouldn't stop there. You can serve chutney as a condiment with any meat, fish, or fowl. Replace cranberry sauce with an apricot chutney at your next holiday dinner if you like. I think chutneys go particularly well with simple roasted or grilled dishes.

And then there is chutney and cheese on crackers, chutney with Chinese eggrolls, chutney-flavored mayonnaise . . .

There's really no excuse for not making enough relishes and chutneys. If you have a food processor, the laborious chore of chopping all those fruits and vegetables disappears. The recipes are very easy to follow — just chop up the vegetables, combine with the spices and vinegar, and cook on top of the stove. Relishes are cooked just briefly, if at all. Chutneys are slowly simmered to blend the complex flavors. Then it's all packed into jars and quickly processed to provide a good seal.

You don't even have to process these wonderful relishes and chutneys. If you can eat them within a week or two, feel free to skip the processing.

SPECIAL TIPS FOR MAKING RELISHES AND CHUTNEYS

Most of the rules for making crisp pickles also apply to making relishes. Start with the freshest, crisp vegetables and you will make wonderfully crunchy relishes. Briefly salt-brining such vegetables as cabbages and summer squash will remove excess water, creating a crisper relish.

Those are the rules; but here are the exceptions. If you use less than perfect vegetables in your relishes, few people will ever notice it. So if your corn is getting a little old or if your tomatoes are overripe, by all means, make a relish. You can even make relishes from frozen vegetables.

The same is true for chutneys. You can use less than perfect fruits for chutneys. You can actually use canned, frozen, or even dried and reconstituted fruit. It will all taste wonderful.

If you are on a special diet, you can skip the salt in these recipes without affecting its safety. Only the Piccalilli requires a salt-brine. Skip this step, or rinse the vegetables to remove all traces of salt before proceeding with the recipe. In most recipes, the salt rounds out the flavor and adds depth to the taste, so experiment before eliminating the salt if possible.

If you aren't familiar with canning, please refer to chapter 2 for the basics.

• RELISH AND CHUTNEY RECIPES •

SWEET HONEY CORN RELISH

This is a sweet one . . .

In a large nonaluminum saucepan, combine the corn, onions, red and green peppers, honey, vinegar, celery seeds, salt, and cayenne. Bring to a boil. While the corn mixture heats, combine the cornstarch and remaining ¼ cup vinegar and stir until smooth. When the corn mixture comes to a boil, stir in the cornstarch mixture. Cook until the mixture thickens, about 5 minutes.

Ladle the hot relish into hot, sterilized pint jars, leaving ¼ inch headspace. Seal. Process in a boiling water bath or steam canner for 5 minutes. Adjust seals if necessary. Store in a cool, dry place.

8	cups raw corn kernels (approximately 12 ears)
2	onions, finely chopped
1	sweet green pepper, finely chopped
1	sweet red pepper, finely chopped
1¼-1½	cups honey
3	cups cider vinegar
1	teaspoon celery seeds
1	tablespoon salt
½	teaspoon cayenne pepper
2	tablespoons cornstarch
¼	cup cider vinegar

YIELD: **5 pints**

CHILI CORN RELISH

2   tablespoons butter
2   tablespoons chili powder
3   garlic cloves, minced
6   cups raw corn kernels
     (4–5 ears)
2   fresh hot peppers,
     chopped
2   green peppers, chopped
1   cup diced celery
3   cups cider vinegar
½   teaspoon salt
½   teaspoon pepper

YIELD: 4 pints

There's plenty of specialty food producers selling freshly ground chili powder. If you haven't already discovered how much better the fresh spice tastes compared to the supermarket variety, please seek it out. A good chili powder elevates this recipe into an extraordinary relish.

In a large saucepan, melt the butter. Add the chili powder and simmer until the chili powder foams, about 5 minutes. Add the garlic, corn, hot peppers, green peppers, and celery and sauté briefly—just long enough to coat all the vegetables with the chili powder. Add the vinegar, salt, and pepper and bring to a boil. Remove from the heat.

Ladle the hot relish into hot sterilized jars, leaving ¼ inch head space. Seal. Process in a boiling water bath or steam canner for 5 minutes. Adjust seals if necessary. Let cool undisturbed for 12 hours. Store in a cool, dry place.

PICCALILLI

A Pennsylvania Dutch classic . . .

A food processor makes the chopping of the vegetables easy. Use the shredding blade for the cabbage, but chop the other vegetables with the steel blade.

Combine the green tomatoes, cabbage, green peppers, and onions in a large nonaluminum bowl. Toss with the salt. Cover with cold water and set aside for about 3 hours. Then drain well.

In a large nonaluminum kettle, combine the vinegar, honey, mustard seeds, ginger, and black pepper. Bring to a boil. Add the drained vegetables, mix well, and simmer for 3–4 minutes. Pack into clean, hot pint jars, leaving ¼ inch head space. Seal. Process in a boiling water bath or steam canner for 5 minutes. Adjust seals if necessary. Let cool undisturbed for 12 hours. Store in a cool, dry place.

4 ½ cups finely chopped green tomatoes (about 20 tomatoes)

12 cups finely chopped or shredded green cabbage

3 green peppers, finely chopped

6 onions, finely chopped

4 tablespoons salt

Water to cover

2 ¼ cups cider vinegar

1 ½ cups honey

1 tablespoon mustard seeds

1 tablespoon ground ginger

1 teaspoon black pepper

YIELD: **6 pints**

JELLIED CRANBERRY RELISH

2   (12-ounce) packages fresh
     or frozen cranberries
2⅔   cups honey
1   cup water
2   apples, quartered
2   tablespoons lemon juice

YIELD: 7 half-pints

This is a holiday classic. If large numbers gather around your Thanksgiving table, you may want to pack the relish in pint jars.

Combine all the ingredients in a large nonaluminum kettle. Bring to a boil and cook until the cranberries are quite soft, 15–20 minutes. Strain through a food mill. Return the strained pulp to the kettle and bring to a boil. Boil for about 2 minutes.

Ladle the hot relish into clean hot half-pint or pint jars, leaving ½ inch head space. Seal. Process in a boiling water bath or steam canner for 10 minutes. Adjust seals if necessary. Let cool undisturbed for 12 hours. Store in a cool, dry place.

HORSERADISH RELISH

If you grow your own horseradish, harvest the roots when the plant is dormant — in late fall or early spring. If you must buy your horseradish, look for it in the supermarkets in the spring.

Peel the root and cut into 1-inch pieces. Place the horseradish root in a food processor fitted with a steel blade. Process until the root is completely shredded. (You can grate the root by hand, but the fumes are near deadly!)

Through the feed tube, add 4 tablespoons vinegar and 4 tablespoons water. Process until mixed. Or mix in by hand. Loosen the top of the processor and allow the fumes to dissipate for about 30 seconds — otherwise be prepared for an intense sensation when the fumes reach your sinuses. Scrape down the sides of the mixing bowl, and check the texture of the relish. If the relish seems dry, add the additional vinegar and water.

Quickly pack the horseradish into a clean jar and seal tightly. Store in the refrigerator. To maintain the hot flavor, expose the horseradish to as little air as possible.

1   **large horseradish root**
4–6 **tablespoons white vinegar**
4–6 **tablespoons water**

YIELD: **1–1½ pints**

FAST CHILI SAUCE

12 pounds tomatoes, cored
and quartered (about 6
quarts)
1 cup cider vinegar
4 onions, quartered
4 green peppers, seeded and
quartered
About 16 jalapeños,
seeded and halved
8 celery ribs, chopped
4 garlic cloves
¼ cup oil
4 tablespoons chili powder
4 tablespoons ground cumin
1½ tablespoons dry mustard
1½ tablespoons oregano

YIELD: 5 quarts

I call this fast because it takes very little handling to get it started. No peeling or straining the tomatoes — although you could do both if you are particular about a little skin or a few seeds floating in the sauce. Although the sauce simmers on the stove for a couple of hours, during that time you are free to be elsewhere — just give the sauce a stir from time to time to prevent scorching.

This chili sauce makes a flavorful catsup substitute, not to mention a wonderful base for nachos, a convenient sauce for tacos, and a delicious addition to refried beans.

Combine the tomatoes and vinegar in a heavy saucepan and cook, covered, until the tomatoes become quite soft, 15–20 minutes.

While the tomatoes cook, finely chop each vegetable, separately, in a food processor fitted with a steel blade. If you do not have a food processor, you can chop by hand — a somewhat more time-consuming task.

In a heavy saucepan, heat the oil. Add the chili powder and cumin and simmer until the chili powder foams, about 5 minutes. Add the chopped vegetables and sauté until the vegetables are slightly tender, about 5 minutes. Remove from the heat.

By now the tomatoes should be very soft. Puree the tomatoes in the food processor or blender until smooth. Add the tomatoes to the vegetables. Add the mustard and oregano. Bring to a boil and simmer until the sauce thickens, 3 hours or more, depending on how ripe and juicy your tomatoes are. Taste and adjust seasonings. No salt is necessary, but it can be added if desired.

Ladle the hot sauce into clean, hot quart jars, leaving ½ inch head space. Seal. Process in a boiling water bath for 10 minutes. Adjust seals if necessary. Cool undisturbed for 12 hours. Store in a cool, dry place. Do not open the jars for 6 weeks to allow the flavors to develop.

CURRY ONION RELISH

4   cups finely chopped
     onions
2½   cups finely chopped sweet
     red peppers
2   cups finely chopped sweet
     green peppers
1   tablespoon finely chopped
     hot pepper
2   cups white vinegar
½   cup white sugar
1   teaspoon mustard seeds
1   teaspoon turmeric
½   teaspoon mace
½   teaspoon ginger
1   teaspoon salt

YIELD: 4½–5 pints

I like to blend my own spices to give this relish a very mild curry flavor.

Combine all the ingredients in a large kettle. Bring to a boil and simmer uncovered for 30 minutes, stirring occasionally. Pack into clean, hot jars, leaving ¼ inch head space. Seal. Process in a boiling water bath for 10 minutes. Cool undisturbed for 12 hours. Store in a cool, dry place.

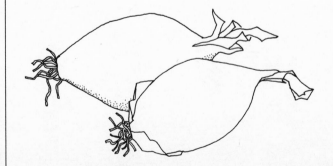

TOMATO CATSUP

It tastes just like quality store-bought catsup. The secret lies in using corn syrup for sweetener—a tip I learned from author Janet Chadwick.

In a large, heavy saucepan, combine the tomatoes, onions, and vinegar. Bring to a boil and continue boiling, covered, until the tomatoes are quite soft, 15–20 minutes.

Puree the tomatoes and onions in a blender or food processor. You will have to do this in several batches. Return to the saucepan and add the remaining ingredients. Simmer over a very low flame until the mixture is reduced by half and is quite thick. This will take 6–8 hours. Stir occasionally to prevent scorching.

Ladle the hot catsup into clean hot pint jars, leaving ½ inch head space. Seal. Process in a boiling water bath or steam canner for 15 minutes. Adjust seals if necessary. Let cool for 12 hours. Store in a cool, dry place.

6	quarts chopped tomatoes
4	onions, chopped
3	cups cider vinegar
12	ounces tomato paste
1	cup light corn syrup
2	teaspoons Tabasco Sauce
2	teaspoons fennel seeds
1	teaspoon whole allspice
1	teaspoon mustard seeds
1	teaspoon celery seeds
2	teaspoons salt
2	teaspoons black pepper

YIELD: 8 pints

SIMPLE SALSA

24 cups quartered ripe tomatoes
2 cups white or cider vinegar
2 onions, finely minced
4 garlic cloves, minced
1¼ cups finely minced hot peppers

YIELD: 4 pints

Salsas are great to eat with eggs, meats, sandwiches, chips, you name it. I use salsas as seasoning bases and as a table relish. This salsa requires very little fussing, so it is ideal to make during the harvest season. It is a hot one—substitute sweet green pepper for some of the hot pepper, if you prefer.

In a large nonaluminum saucepan, combine the tomatoes and vinegar. Bring to a boil and simmer until the tomatoes are very soft, about 45 minutes.

While the tomatoes cook, prepare the other vegetables. A food processor can be used to mince each vegetable separately.

When the tomatoes are very soft, process them through a food mill or strainer to remove the seeds and skins. Return to the saucepan, and add the minced vegetables. Simmer until the salsa has reduced to a nice thick sauce, about 1 hour.

Ladle the hot salsa into clean hot half-pint or pint jars, leaving ¼ inch head space. Seal. Process in a boiling water bath or steam canner for 15 minutes. Adjust seals if necessary. Let cool undisturbed for 12 hours. Store in a cool, dry place. Do not open jars for 6 weeks to allow the flavors to develop.

ZUCCHINI HOT DOG RELISH

The horseradish and hot peppers give this relish a hot flavor. It doesn't taste like a traditional hot dog relish, but it seems to beg to be served with hot dogs.

In a large bowl, combine the zucchini, onions, peppers, and salt. Mix well. Cover with cold water. Let stand overnight.

Rinse the vegetables well and drain in a colander. Weight the vegetables with a heavy plate and allow to drain for at least 30 minutes.

In a large kettle, combine the vinegar, horseradish, honey, mace, and turmeric. Bring to a boil. Add the vegetables. Return to a boil. While the vegetables heat, combine the cornstarch and water. Stir to form a smooth paste. Stir the cornstarch into the vegetables. Continue to cook until the mixture thickens, about 5 minutes. Do not overcook.

Ladle the hot relish into clean, hot pint or half-pint jars, leaving ½ inch headspace. Seal. Process in a boiling water bath or steam canner for 5 minutes. Adjust seals at once. Let cool undisturbed for 12 hours. Store in a cool, dry place.

8	packed cups grated zucchini
2	cups chopped onions
4	hot peppers, chopped
2	tablespoons salt
	Water
1 ¾	cups white vinegar
2	tablespoons prepared horseradish
¼	cup honey
1	teaspoon mace
1	teaspoon turmeric
2	tablespoons cornstarch
½	cup water

YIELD: About 4 pints

APRICOT DATE CHUTNEY

2½   pounds apricots
10   garlic cloves
2   inch cube fresh ginger
1   cup cider vinegar
1   cup honey
½   teaspoon cayenne pepper
¼   teaspoon salt
¼   teaspoon cinnamon
1   cup chopped dates

YIELD: **About 6 half-pints**

I never make enough of this chutney because I give so many jars away. This mild, garlicky chutney is particularly nice with lamb and chicken dishes.

Blanch the apricots by immersing in boiling water to cover for 30 seconds. Peel, remove the pits, and chop finely. A food processor does this job easily; do not overprocess.

Finely mince the garlic. Peel and finely mince the ginger. These can be minced together in the food processor.

Combine the apricots, garlic, ginger, vinegar, honey, cayenne, salt, and cinnamon in a large, nonaluminum saucepan. Bring to a boil, then simmer, partially covered, for 30 minutes. Stir occasionally. Add the dates and continue to simmer for another 30 minutes. Stir frequently as the chutney scorches easily.

Ladle the hot chutney into clean, hot half-pint jars, leaving ¼ inch headspace. Seal. Process for 10 minutes in a boiling water bath. Store in a cool, dry place.

PEACH ORANGE CHUTNEY

Blanch the peaches in boiling water to cover for 30 seconds. Peel, remove the pits, and chop finely. A food processor does this job nicely. Do not overprocess. Pour the peaches into a large pot.

Peel the orange, being careful to peel off just the thin orange rind. Combine the orange rind with the ginger root in the food processor and process until finely minced. You can do this job by hand also. Add to the peaches.

Remove the white membrane from the orange and discard. Chop the orange, remove any pits, and add to the peaches. Add the remaining ingredients, bring to a boil, and simmer uncovered for 2–3 hours, stirring occasionally. The chutney will thicken and reduce.

Ladle the hot chutney into clean, hot half-pint jars, leaving ¼ inch head space. Process for 10 minutes. Adjust seals if necessary. Let cool undisturbed for 12 hours. Store in a cool, dry place.

2 ½	pounds peaches
1	orange
2	inch cube fresh ginger root
1	cup cider vinegar
1	cup honey
½	teaspoon cayenne pepper
¼	teaspoon turmeric
⅛	teaspoon ground coriander

YIELD: **About 6 half-pints**

PLUM CHUTNEY

6   pounds Italian prune plums

2   onions, chopped

4   garlic cloves, minced

1   cup cider vinegar

¾   cup honey

2   teaspoons Chinese five spice powder (available at oriental and specialty food stores)

½   teaspoon cayenne pepper

YIELD: **5 half-pints**

This sweet and sour sauce is delicious as a dipping sauce for eggrolls.

Plunge the plums into boiling water for 1 minute to loosen the skins. Peel and pit the plums.

In a nonaluminum saucepan, combine the plums with the remaining ingredients. Simmer until the mixture becomes a smooth sauce, about 1 hour. As the chutney cooks, break up the plums with a spoon and stir frequently to avoid scorching.

Ladle the hot chutney into clean, hot half-pint jars, leaving ¼ inch head space. Seal. Process in a boiling water bath or steam canner for 10 minutes. Adjust seals if necessary. Cool undisturbed for 12 hours. Store in a cool, dry place.

· 5 ·

Salt-brined Pickles
By the Jar & By the Crock

The art of pickling in salt goes way back. The Chinese and other people of the Orient have been doing it for centuries. Some would say that the craft of making pickles has reached its pinnacle in the barrels of kosher dills, sauerkraut, and pickled peppers that line Essex Street in the Lower East Side of New York City.

A visitor to Essex Street is struck by the pungent odor of garlic and dill wafting above the barrels. A single pickle is fished out of the barrel by a bare-armed man and slipped into a waxed paper bag for eating on the spot. A pound or more of sauerkraut is weighed out and sold in a plastic container. The flavors are exquisite; the variety of pickles amazing.

There are dill pickles sold "green," just barely fermented—a delicate white-green with the flavor of dill only slightly stronger than the garlic. Next to the barrel of green pickles are the half-sours, then the three-quarter sours, then the very sharp-flavored olive-green sour dills.

These pickles set the standards by which most people judge their dill pickles. You can make similar pickles at home.

The Process of Fermentation

Salt-cured pickles are made from raw vegetables, salt, water, and spices. The salt draws liquid from the raw vegetables and acts as a preservative. When cabbages are salted, they release enough water normally to create their own brine. Cucumbers release less liquid so they must be covered with water. Naturally occurring bacteria convert sugars in the raw vegetables into lactic acid. Lactic acid is smoother tasting than acetic acid (vinegar) and gives fermented pickles their distinctive flavor. Generous amounts of spices and herbs round out the flavor.

The stronger the salt concentration in the brine, the longer the pickles will keep. But the stronger the salt concentration, the saltier the pickle tastes. Indeed, it used to be the custom to preserve cucumbers in a 10 percent brine (1½ cups of salt to 9 pints water), strong enough to float an egg and prevent the growth of most bacteria. The resulting pickle was so salty it had to be rinsed in several changes of water over the course of several days before it was edible. I do not use a 10 percent brine for any pickle recipe.

The pickles in this cookbook are mostly cured in a 2½ percent to 3 percent low-salt brine. Generally, a low-salt brine enables the fermentation to begin quickly, but it ends quickly as well. Some pickles are ready to eat in about 3 days, others take 10–14 days to be full flavored. Once a pickle has been sufficiently cured, it must be refrigerated or processed in a boiling water bath or steam canner to prevent it from spoiling.

PREPARING THE PICKLING CROCK

Any large glass or stoneware crock or gallon jar can be used for making fermented pickles. To prepare the crock, it must be thoroughly washed with hot, soapy water and rinsed well. To eliminate any undesirable bacteria which can ruin your pickles, it is a good idea to scald the crock by rinsing again with boiling water.

PREPARING THE VEGETABLES

Besides cucumbers and cabbages, excellent choices for fermented pickles include green beans, green tomatoes, okra, turnips, onions, and even corn.

The vegetables should be well scrubbed and drained before being placed in the pickle crock. Be sure to scrub off the blossom end on cucumbers, which contains enzymes that may spoil the pickles.

Start with the freshest, juiciest vegetables. A cabbage that has been stored for too long may not contain enough moisture to create its own brine. Although you can add more 2½ percent brine to cabbage that does not create enough brine, fermentation will not go as smoothly as it does with juicy fresh cabbage.

PACKING THE CROCK

Start with grape leaves, if you will be using them, and line the bottom of the crock. Add the spices, then the vegetables. The vegetables will hold the spices under the surface of the brine. When packing cucumbers, pack the smaller ones on the bottom so the larger cucumbers will hold them down. Leave several inches of space at the top of the crock.

Prepare the brine carefully, following the recipe directions. Measure the pickling salt and water exactly. More or less spices and herbs won't make much difference.

Covering Vegetables with Brine

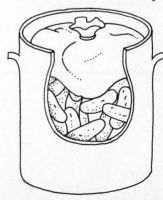

Vegetables Weighted down with a Plastic Bag

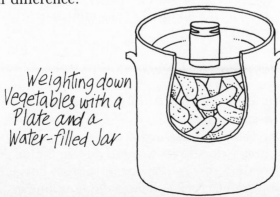

Weighting down Vegetables with a Plate and a Water-filled Jar

Pour the brine over the vegetables, being sure that the brine *completely covers the vegetables*. There should be about 4 inches of space above the top of the brine. Weight the vegetables with a heavy plate to be sure that everything is submerged beneath the brine. A glass jar filled with water can weight the plate. With sauerkraut and sauerruben (made from turnips) exclude air from the surface of the vegetables by filling a plastic bag with water and placing the bag over the vegetables.

Cover the entire crock with plastic wrap to prevent dust and air-borne molds from settling in the crock.

FERMENTATION TAKES 3 DAYS TO SEVERAL WEEKS

The ideal fermentation temperature is about 68° F. Set your pickling crock where the ideal temperature can be met as closely as possible. Do not set the crock where the temperature fluctuates widely. The colder the temperature where the pickling crock is located, the slower the fermentation.

Fermentation should begin within a few days. You will notice air bubbles escaping from the crock. A distinctively sharp, but not unpleasant, smell should rise from the crock. Check the crock daily and remove any scum that forms on the top.

With a low-salt brine, the fermentation will be completed in about 3 days. The pickles will be green or half-sour at this stage. Refrigerate the pickles when they have been cured to your satisfaction. Other pickles will ferment for about 2 weeks, and sauerkraut usually takes 4–6 weeks to cure.

Keeping Fermented Pickles

You can keep fermented pickles in the refrigerator or you can process the pickles in canning jars.

If the fermentation has proceeded well, you can put the pickles and fermentation brine directly into the refrigerator. The process has gone well when the fermentation begins within a day or so of combining the ingredients in the crock and lasts about as long as the recipe specifies. The brine will be clear and tasty, not cloudy or slightly funky tasting.

If the pickles taste good and have a good firm texture, but the brine is slightly cloudy, drain off the brine (reserving it) and strain out the spices. Bring the reserved brine to a boil and cool to room temperature. Pack the pickles into clean quart jars. Add fresh spices. Pour the cooled brine over the pickles and refrigerate. These pickles will keep for at least several months.

If you want to process the pickles for long-term storage, drain off the brine (reserving it) and strain out the spices. Bring the reserved brine to a boil in a nonaluminum saucepan. Pack fresh spices and the cucumbers into hot sterilized jars. See chapter 2 for information on preparing jars and lids.

Pour the hot brine over the pickles, leaving ½ inch head space. Process in a boiling water bath or steam canner for 5 minutes. Adjust seals if necessary. Let cool for 12 hours, then check for seals. See chapter 2 for information on checking seals. Store any unsealed jars in the refrigerator. Label and store the jars in a cool, dry place.

Processing does take away a little of the crispness of your pickles. Obviously, its main advantage is that the jars need not take up valuable refrigerator space.

Sauerkraut

Sauerkraut can be very satisfactorily processed. Heat the sauerkraut in a heavy, nonaluminum saucepan, but do not allow it to come to a boil. Pack the hot sauerkraut into clean, hot jars, leaving ½ inch head space. The sauerkraut should be covered with brine. If you don't have enough brine, mix up a brine of 1½ tablespoons pickling salt to 1 quart water (2½ percent brine). Evenly distribute this fresh brine among the jars. Seal. Process in a boiling water bath or steam canner, pints for 15 minutes, quarts for 20 minutes. Adjust seals if necessary. Let cool undisturbed for 12 hours, then check for seals. Store any unsealed jars in the refrigerator. Label and store the jars in a cool, dry place.

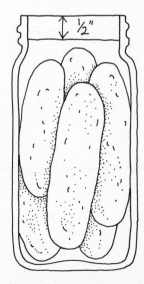

Leave Headspace

WHAT WENT WRONG?

   If your pickles smell bad, if the skins are slippery or gooey, if the brine is perfectly clear with a large quantity of sediment on the bottom of the crock, the pickles have gone bad and they should be thrown out where even the animals won't get to them. If the pickles are good, but not as wonderful as you had hoped, perhaps you can find the reason for your partial success in the chart below.

PROBLEM	*POSSIBLE CAUSE*
Soft pickles	*Brine too weak*
	Not removing the scum daily from brine
	Not submerging pickles beneath brine
	Using hard water
	Blossom ends attached to cucumbers
	Storage area too warm
Shriveled pickles	*Wilted vegetables were used*
	Brine too strong
Hollow pickles	*Temperature too high during fermentation*
	Cucumbers grown under poor conditions
Dark pickles	*Minerals in the water, especially iron*
Excessive white sediment	*Table salt used*
	Bacterial growth in fermentation
	Temperature fluctuations
Spoiled pickles	*Vegetables or crock not well scrubbed*
	Air not adequately excluded from crock
	Brine too weak
	Pickles not refrigerated after fermentation ceased

• SALT-CURED PICKLE RECIPES •

HALF-SOUR PICKLES

If you are looking for a crispy deli pickle, this is the one to make — mildly sour, richly flavored with dill and garlic.

Combine the water and pickling salt in a pickle crock. Stir well to dissolve the salt.

Wash the cucumbers and remove the blossom ends. Drain well. Add the cucumbers to the salted water, mixing in the garlic, dill, hot peppers, and pickling spices with the cucumbers. Stir gently to distribute the spices evenly. Cover with a weight to keep the cucumbers submerged in the brine. Cover the crock.

Store the crock at 68° F. Check the crock every day. Remove any scum that forms on the top. The pickles should be "half-sour" in about 3 days. Taste the pickles. If the results are pleasing, prepare the pickles for long-term storage.

Pack the pickles in sterilized quart jars. Pour the brine into a nonaluminum pan and bring to a boil. Boil for 5 minutes. Cool to room temperature. Pour the cooled brine over the pickles, seal the jars, and store in the refrigerator.

Because of the relatively low salt concentration in the brine, the pickles spoil easily if they aren't refrigerated after a week. Don't use this recipe if you are looking for a very sour pickle.

8	cups water
¼	cup pickling salt
1	gallon small pickling cucumbers
6	garlic cloves
6	dill heads or sprigs of fresh dill
2	tablespoons dill seeds
2	small fresh or dried hot peppers
2	tablespoons mixed pickling spices

YIELD: 4 quarts

SMALL-SCALE SAUERKRAUT

9   cups shredded cabbage
¼   cup pickling salt

By the Quart

This is a very simple recipe to make. You can make 2–3 quarts of sauerkraut from 1 head of cabbage. Add spices, such as garlic, dill seed, or juniper berries to the cabbage, if desired.

Trim off the outer leaves of the cabbage and wash the cabbage. Trim off the central core. Thinly shred the cabbage. You can do this with a food processor (use the slicing, not the grating, blade) or a kraut cutting board. As you slice the cabbage, measure out 9 cups into a large bowl.

Mix the cabbage with the pickling salt. Let stand for at least 2 hours. Rinse, drain, and rinse again. With water still clinging to the cabbage, pack into sterilized quart jars. Pack firmly and keep tamping down on the surface of the cabbage until liquid rises to cover the top of the cabbage. Leave at least 1 inch of head space at the top of the jar; more space is okay.

Wipe away any stray pieces of cabbage from the inside of the jar. Fit a piece of plastic wrap on top of the cabbage to exclude air from reaching the cabbage. Seal with a 2-piece metal canning lid, but do not tighten the screwband.

Store the packed jar in a room where the temperature stays at 68–72°
F. This is the ideal temperature for fermentation. Check the sauerkraut
from time to time and remove any scum that appears on the surface.
There should be no scum forming if the plastic wrap is excluding air
properly. Fermentation should cease after 2–6 weeks.

You can tell when the sauerkraut is ready. There will be no more air
bubbles at the surface of the kraut, and the jar will not release a hiss
of gas when you remove the screwband. The kraut will smell pungently
pickled. It may taste too salty. If it is too salty for your taste, rinse
the kraut before you serve it. If possible, do not rinse more than you
plan to serve at one time. Store the sauerkraut in the refrigerator.

TARRAGON HALF-SOURS

1   gallon water
¼   cup pickling salt
1   gallon small pickling
      cucumbers
¼ – ½ cup fresh tarragon leaves
2   tablespoons mixed
      pickling spices
1   inch piece horseradish

YIELD: 4 quarts

Tired of the same old dill pickles? Try using tarragon in the crock, instead of dill. The flavor is wonderful — if you like the anise taste tarragon lends to foods.

Combine the water and pickling salt in the pickling crock. Stir well to dissolve the salt.

Wash the cucumbers well. Remove the blossom ends. Drain.

Add the cucumbers to the pickling crock, along with the tarragon, pickling spices, and horseradish. Stir gently to distribute the spices evenly. Weight the cucumbers with a heavy plate to keep them submerged in the brine. Cover the crock with a heavy plate.

Store the crock at 68° F. Check each day and remove any scum that forms. Taste the pickles after 3 days. They should be at the "green stage." If the results are pleasing, prepare the cucumbers for long-term storage. Since the tarragon flavor intensifies into a very strong licorice taste, I recommend that you stop the fermentation at this point.

Pack the pickles into sterilized quart jars. Strain the brine, and discard the spices, and bring to a boil. Boil for about 5 minutes. Cool to room temperature. Pour the cooled brine over the pickles and seal the jars. Store these pickles in the refrigerator.

CROCK DILLY BEANS

These are my favorite dilly beans: garlicky, crisp, strongly flavored. They are the easiest dilly beans to make.

Combine the water and pickling salt in the pickling crock. Stir well to dissolve the salt.

Wash the beans and trim off the stem ends. Drain. Add to the pickling crock, along with the dill, garlic, mustard seeds, bay leaves, and horseradish. Stir gently to distribute the spices. Cover with a weight to keep the beans submerged in the brine. Cover the crock and store at 68° F.

Check the crock every few days and remove any scum that forms on the top. The beans will be well pickled after 10 days: crisp, firm, olive green in color, and strongly flavored. If the beans are not crisp, if they are slimy to the touch, if they don't smell good, throw them out. But chances are, the fermentation went well.

Sterilize 4 quart jars. Pack the beans up to the neck of the jars. Strain the brine. Bring to a boil in a nonaluminum pan and boil for 5 minutes. Cool to room temperature. Pour over the beans, leaving about ½ inch head space. Seal and store in the refrigerator.

1	gallon water
½	cup pickling salt
4	pounds green beans (about 1 gallon)
4	dill heads or sprigs of dill weed
6	garlic cloves
1	tablespoon mustard seeds
2	bay leaves
1	inch piece horseradish

YIELD: 4 quarts

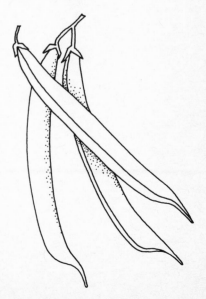

LARGE-SCALE SAUERKRAUT

45 pounds cabbage
1 pound pickling salt

YIELD: 5 gallons

This recipe should be made in a 5-gallon stoneware crock. You will need a scale for this.

First prepare the crock according to directions on page 84.

Trim off the outer leaves of the cabbage and wash the cabbages. Trim off the central core. Thinly shred the cabbage. You can do this with a food processor (use the slicing, not the grating, blade) or a kraut cutting board. As you slice the cabbage, measure out 5 pounds of cabbage into a large pan.

Mix the first 5 pounds of cabbage with 3 tablespoons of pickling salt. Slice more cabbage. Add the second 5 pounds of cabbage and 3 more tablespoons of pickling salt to the large pan. Mix well. Continue slicing and mixing until you have sliced all the cabbage and added all the pickling salt.

Begin packing the cabbage into the clean 5-gallon crock. Pack in a layer at a time, tamping down firmly to remove any air bubbles and to bruise the cabbage so it releases more juice. Continue filling and tamping. You should be able to draw enough juice from the cabbage to cover the cabbage in liquid. There should be at least 4 inches of space left at the top of the crock.

Wipe away any stray pieces of cabbage from the inside of the crock. Fit a large food-safe plastic bag on top of the cabbage. Fill with water. This will keep out any air, which could spoil the fermentation process.

Store the sauerkraut crock in a room where the temperature stays at 68–72° F. This is the ideal temperature for fermentation. Check the sauerkraut from time to time and remove any scum that appears on the surface. There should be no scum forming if the bag is excluding air properly. Fermentation should cease after 4–6 weeks. You can tell when the sauerkraut is ready. There will be no more air bubbles at the surface of the kraut. The kraut will smell pungently pickled.

Sauerkraut can be kept in the refrigerator, or you can process it for long-term storage. Heat the sauerkraut to simmering, but do not bring it to a boil. Pack the kraut into clean, hot quart jars, leaving ½ inch headspace. Make sure the kraut is covered with brine. If there isn't enough brine, mix up more 2½ percent brine (1½ tablespoons pickling salt to 1 quart water) and evenly distribute it among the jars. Seal. Process in a boiling water bath or steam canner for 20 minutes. Let cool undisturbed for 12 hours. Store in a cool, dry place.

KIMCHEE I

8 cups Chinese cabbage or bok choy, cut in 1½ inch pieces

½ cup pickling salt

Water to cover

¾ cup julienne-sliced daikon (Japanese white radish) or turnip

¼ cup julienne-sliced carrots

2 garlic cloves, minced

2 teaspoons chili paste with garlic

½ teaspoon minced fresh ginger root

¼ teaspoon sugar

By the Quart

Kimchee is a peppery hot fermented cabbage pickle that comes from Korea, where it is served with plenty of rice. I normally serve kimchee as a condiment. This version isn't very hot, but it does leave a pleasant glow in the mouth.

The chili paste with garlic and the daikon are both available in oriental food stores.

In a large bowl, combine the cabbage and pickling salt. Mix to evenly distribute the salt. Add water to cover. Let stand for 2 hours. Rinse well and drain, leaving some water clinging to the cabbage. Stir in the remaining ingredients.

Pack the mixture into a hot, clean 1-quart canning jar. Cover with a 2-piece canning lid; do not tighten the screwband. Let the Kimchee stand in a cool place for 3–5 days, depending on how strongly flavored you want it to taste. Store in the refrigerator. It will keep for several months.

KIMCHEE II

This kimchee is much hotter than the preceding one — hot enough to be best enjoyed on top of rice and served with a mouth-cooling beer.

In a large bowl, combine the Chinese cabbage, green cabbage, and pickling salt. Mix to evenly distribute the salt. Add water to cover. Let stand for 2 hours. Rinse well and drain, leaving some water clinging to the cabbage. Stir in the remaining ingredients.

Tightly pack the mixture into a hot, clean 1-quart canning jar. Cover with a 2-piece canning lid; do not tighten the screwband. Let the kimchee stand in a cool place for 5–10 days, depending on how strongly flavored you want it. For long-term storage, store covered in the refrigerator or very cool cellar. It will keep for several months.

4	cups Chinese cabbage, cut in 1½ inch pieces
2	cups green cabbage, cut in 1½ inch pieces
½	cup pickling salt
	Water to cover
1	jalapeño (or similar fresh hot pepper), seeded and sliced
1	cup julienne-sliced carrots
1	cup julienne-sliced daikon (Japanese white radish) or turnip
4	green onions, including the green tops, sliced in 1½ inch pieces
1	teaspoon grated fresh ginger root
2	garlic cloves, minced
1	teaspoon cayenne pepper
1	teaspoon sugar

By the Quart

CROCK GREEN TOMATOES

3   quarts water
½   cup pickling salt
3   quarts green tomatoes
4   garlic cloves
4   bay leaves
6   dill heads or
     6 tablespoons dill seeds
1   tablespoon mixed pickling
     spices
4   cups white vinegar
1⅓   cups water
3   teaspoons pickling salt
6   garlic cloves
6   tablespoons dill seed
3   bay leaves

YIELD: 3 quarts

When that killing frost threatens, it is easy to throw some green tomatoes in a crock with some salt, spices, and water and make delicious pickles. In fact, these tomatoes are so delicious, you might find yourself harvesting green tomatoes all summer long. Select the firmest, least ripe tomatoes—any variety will do. For long-term storage and the best flavor, I recommend processing the finished pickles in a steam canner or boiling water bath.

Combine the 3 quarts water and ½ cup pickling salt in the pickling crock. Stir well to dissolve the salt.

Wash the tomatoes and drain well. Do not bother to remove the stems. Add to the pickling crock, along with 4 garlic cloves, 4 bay leaves, 6 dill heads or 6 tablespoons dill seeds, and 1 tablespoon mixed pickling spices. Stir gently to distribute the spices. Cover with a weight to keep the tomatoes submerged in the brine. Cover the crock and store at 68° F.

Check the crock every few days and remove any scum that forms on the top. The tomatoes will be well pickled after about 10 days. They should be crisp, firm, olive green in color, and strongly flavored. I have found that the tomatoes improve in flavor if they are processed in a new brine at this point; so if the tomatoes don't taste exactly as you had hoped, don't be discouraged. However, if the tomatoes do not smell good or are slimy to the touch, throw them out. But chances are, the fermentation went well, and you're on your way to some fine pickles.

Sterilize 3 quart jars. Drain the tomatoes and discard the fermentation brine. To prepare a new brine, combine the remaining 4 cups white vinegar, 1 ⅓ cups water, and 3 teaspoons pickling salt. Heat to boiling.

While the brine heats, pack each sterilized jar with 2 garlic cloves, 2 tablespoons dill seeds, and 1 bay leaf. Pack with the tomatoes, leaving at least ½ inch head space. Pack tightly, without squashing any of the tomatoes. Pour the hot brine over the tomatoes, leaving ½ inch head space. Seal. Process in a boiling water bath or steam canner for 5 minutes. Adjust seals, if necessary. Let cool undisturbed for 12 hours. Store in a cool dry place.

SALT-CURED CARROTS

1   quart carrot sticks (about 3 pounds)
2   garlic cloves
2   bay leaves
¼   teaspoon whole allspice
1   tablespoon pickling salt
1   cup white wine vinegar
      Water to cover

By the Quart

These carrots make a delicious addition to antipasto plates and salads. I like to eat them straight out of the jar for a snack.

Pack the carrots, garlic, bay leaves and allspice into a clean quart jar. Mix together the pickling salt and vinegar and pour over the carrots. Add water to cover.

Cover the jar but do not screw down the lid too firmly. Set the jar in a room where the temperature remains between 60° F. and 70° F. for 10–14 days. Fermentation is completed when the carrots all sink to the bottom of the jar. If you tap the jar, no bubbles should rise to the top. Store in the refrigerator.

· 6 ·

Quick & Easy
Freezer Pickles

Freezer pickles aren't "true" pickles, but they offer such a wonderful, fast way to preserve cucumbers that I couldn't leave them out. Freezer pickles taste more like a marinated cucumber than a pickle. You can serve them as pickles—or you can add them to your winter salads.

The process of making freezer pickles is quite simple. Your actual preparation time will be 20 minutes or less. If you are working with large quantities of cucumbers, simply double or triple the recipes. But I think the real advantage of freezer pickles is that you can make them in small quantities, as your cucumbers ripen.

The first step is to salt the cucumbers (or cabbage) to draw out any excess water. Then you rinse and drain the cucumbers. It is important to rinse the cucumbers; otherwise they will probably taste too salty. Taste the cucumbers after you have rinsed them. If they still taste too salty, rinse again. Then combine the cucumbers with a brine that has some white vinegar (for the best color), sugar, and spices.

The pickles are then packed into freezer containers, leaving about 1 inch head space for expansion in the freezer. I prefer to use plastic feezer containers for these pickles, but plastic freezer bags work just as well, although they are awkward to handle once the pickles are defrosted.

Defrosting should be done in the refrigerator for best flavor and texture. It will take about 8 hours to defrost. Once defrosted, the pickles will keep for weeks in the refrigerator; that is, if they last that long.

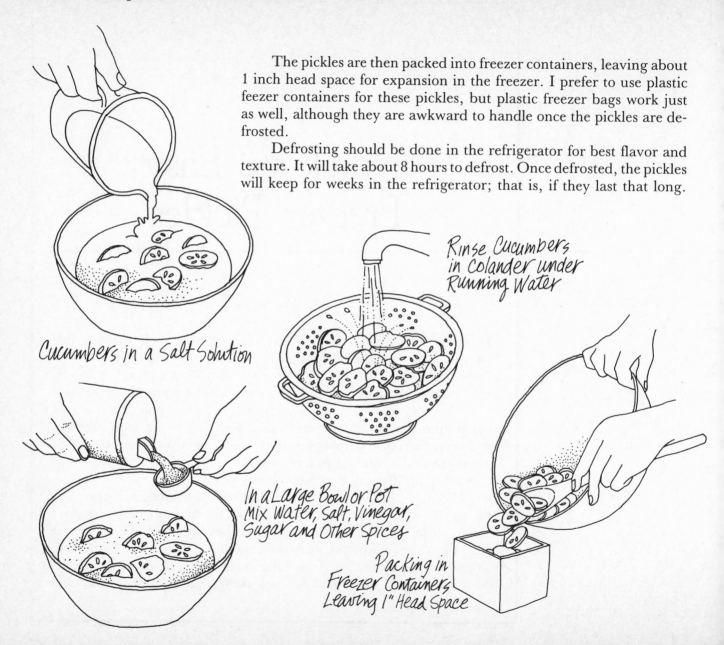

Cucumbers in a Salt Solution

Rinse Cucumbers in Colander under Running Water

In a Large Bowl or Pot Mix Water, Salt, Vinegar, Sugar and Other Spices

Packing in Freezer Containers Leaving 1" Head Space

FREEZER DILLS

This recipe makes a sweet, subtly flavored dill pickle.

In a large nonaluminum bowl, combine the cucumbers, garlic, and pickling salt. Cover with water. Set aside for at least 3 hours. Then drain, rinse, and drain the cucumbers again.

Combine the white vinegar and sugar. Stir to dissolve the sugar. Add the cucumbers and toss to coat well.

Place the dill, dill seed, and bay leaf into the freezer container. Add the cucumbers and pickling liquid, leaving at least 1 inch head space. Close tightly and freeze.

Defrost in the refrigerator for at least 8 hours before serving.

3 ½ cups thinly sliced cucumbers
2 garlic cloves, thinly sliced
1 tablespoon pickling salt
Water
1 cup white vinegar
¼ cup sugar
1 sprig fresh dill
1 teaspoon dill seeds
1 bay leaf

YIELD: About 3 cups

FREEZER BREAD AND BUTTERS

4 cups thinly sliced
   cucumbers
1 onion, thinly sliced
1½ teaspoons pickling salt
1¼ cups white vinegar
½ cup sugar
1 teaspoon turmeric
¼ teaspoon celery seeds
¼ teaspoon black pepper

By the Quart

This brine is similar to a traditional bread and butter, but the end result is different. These pickles taste fresh!

Combine the cucumbers, onion, and pickling salt. Let stand for at least 2 hours. Drain, but do not rinse.

Combine the vinegar, sugar, turmeric, celery seeds, and black pepper. Pour over the cucumbers; the brine will not completely cover the cucumbers, but that's okay. Pack into freezer containers, leaving about 1 inch head space. Freeze.

Defrost in the refrigerator for at least 8 hours before serving.

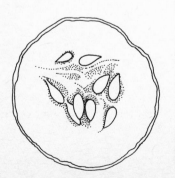

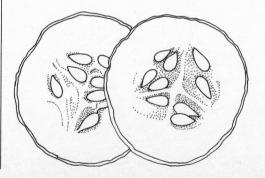

FREEZER LEMON CUCUMBERS

A sweet lemony cucumber — refreshing and distinctive.

Combine the cucumbers, onion, and pickling salt. Let stand for 3–5 hours. Drain, but do not rinse. Add the lemon. Combine the vinegar and sugar and pour over the vegetables. Pack into a freezer container, leaving about 1 inch head space. Freeze.

Defrost for at least 8 hours in the refrigerator before serving.

6	cups thinly sliced cucumbers
1	onion, thinly sliced
1½	teaspoons pickling salt
½	lemon, thinly sliced
1	cup white vinegar
⅔	cup sugar

By the Quart

FREEZER MIXED PICKLES

Combine the cucumbers, onion, pepper, carrot, and pickling salt. Let stand for 3–5 hours. Drain, rinse, and drain again. Combine the vinegar, sugar, and celery seeds. Mix with the vegetables. Spoon the vegetables and brine into freezer containers, leaving at least 1 inch head space. Freeze.

Defrost for at least 8 hours in the refrigerator before serving.

4	cups thinly sliced cucumbers
1	small onion, sliced
½	green pepper, thinly sliced
1	carrot, grated
1	tablespoon pickling salt
1	cup white vinegar
½	cup sugar
1	teaspoon celery seeds

By the Quart

LEMONY TARRAGON FREEZER PICKLES

4   cups thinly sliced cucumbers
1   onion, thinly sliced
1   green pepper, thinly sliced
1½ teaspoons pickling salt
½   lemon, thinly sliced
1   teaspoon fresh or dried tarragon
1¼ cups white vinegar
½   cup sugar

By the Quart

Combine the cucumbers, onion, green pepper, and pickling salt. Let stand for at least 2 hours. Drain, but do not rinse. Add the lemon and tarragon.

Mix together the vinegar and sugar. Pour over the cucumbers. Pack into freezer containers, leaving about 1 inch head space and freeze.

Defrost for at least 8 hours in the refrigerator before serving.

GINGER GARLIC FREEZER PICKLES

The ginger and garlic combination is a favorite in Chinese cooking. These crispy pickles are wonderfully flavored—my favorite among the freezer pickles.

In a large bowl, combine the cucumbers, onion, carrot, garlic, ginger, and pickling salt. Let stand for about 2 hours. Then drain, rinse, and drain again. The cucumbers should still taste of salt.

Combine the vinegar and sugar and stir to dissolve the sugar. Pour over the vegetables. Pack in freezer containers, leaving about 1 inch head space. Freeze.

Defrost in the refrigerator for at least 8 hours before freezing.

3	cups cucumbers, thinly sliced
1	onion, thinly sliced
1	carrot, grated
3	garlic cloves, thinly sliced
2	inch piece fresh ginger root, very thinly sliced
1	tablespoon salt
1	cup vinegar
½	cup sugar

By the Quart

FREEZER CABBAGE RELISH

1	medium-size cabbage, shredded (14–16 cups)
1	onion, thinly sliced
1	green pepper, thinly sliced
2	carrots, shredded
1	tablespoon pickling salt
½	cup sugar
2	teaspoons dry mustard
2	cups cider vinegar

YIELD: **About 6 pints**

Grilled cheese with Freezer Cabbage Relish on rye is a sandwich that has no peer. I like to keep this relish on hand for sandwiches — of all types — when lettuce isn't available.

In a large bowl, combine the cabbage, onion, green pepper, carrots, and pickling salt. Mix well. Set aside for at least 2 hours.

Taste a piece of cabbage. If it is too salty, rinse and drain briefly. (I usually do not rinse the cabbage.)

Prepare the brine by mixing together the sugar and mustard in a small bowl. Stir in the cider. Keep stirring until all is dissolved. Pour over the vegetables. Pack into freezer containers, leaving at least 1 inch head space. Freeze.

Defrost in the refrigerator for at least 8 hours before serving.

· 7 ·

Jams, Preserves, Conserves & Fruit Butters

Nothing is as reminiscent of summer to me as the aroma of a newly opened jar of strawberry jam. Jams, jellies, and all the other fruit preserves, can be made with surprisingly small amounts of sweeteners, so they taste just like the the sun-ripened fruit you started with.

If the idea of making jams and preserves in the heat of the summer doesn't excite you, no problem. Just freeze the fruit without any added sweetener to make it into preserves in the cool fall weather (see chapter 1 for details).

Types of Preserves

Technically, preserves are whole pieces of fruit in a slightly gelled syrup. But the word also has come to include jams, and jellies, and other types of preserved fruits. It's confusing, but I've searched and searched for another term that can encompass jams, jellies, preserves, conserves, marmalades, and butters, and I can't find one. So in this chapter, when I say "preserves" I am usually referring to *all* types of preserves — not just fruit in slightly gelled syrup.

Jams are similar to preserves, but are made from pureed or crushed fruit, not whole fruit. Jams are slightly gelled to have a nice spreading consistency. Conserves are similar to preserves, but they usually include nuts. Butters are made of fruit pulp cooked down to a spreading consistency. Jellies are clear fruit juices that have been gelled to a firm, spreadable consistency. Marmalades are clear jellies in which pieces of fruit, usually citrus fruit, are suspended.

Low-Sugar Preserves Require Special Care

All of the recipes in this chapter, as well as in chapter 8, are low-sugar recipes. Sugar is a natural preservative. Preserves made with the low-sugar recipes in this cookbook will not keep as long, once opened, as preserves made with more sugar. This doesn't mean that your preserves will necessarily go bad on you. It does mean that you should can your preserves in half-pint jars, rather than pint jars, so that you empty each jar quickly. It means that open jars should *always* be stored in the refrigerator. Properly prepared, opened jars of preserves keep at least a month, and usually about 3 months, in the refrigerator without fermenting or becoming moldy.

CANNING LOW-SUGAR PRESERVES

Until quite recently, preserves were made by a method called *open kettle canning*. Quite simply, when a batch of jam, for example, was cooked down, it was ladled into hot, sterilized jars, the lids were secured to the jars, and the screwbands tightened. As the jars cooled, they sealed (usually). A lot of sugar, which protected the jam from spoiling, was used in each recipe.

You can use this method of open kettle canning for firm jellies, but for safety, you should plan to process all your jams, preserves, conserves, marmalades, and butters in a boiling water bath or steam canner. The USDA allows for sealing jellies with paraffin or a 2-piece metal lid and screwband. For extra safety, I usually process my jellies as well, but this precaution may not be necessary.

USE STERILIZED CANNING JARS

The USDA recommends that anytime you process for less than 10 minutes, which is the case with preserves, you should use sterilized jars. For instructions on sterilizing jars, see chapter 2. You must also use sterilized jars if you are sealing with paraffin or using open kettle canning.

Prepare the canning lids according to the manufacturer's suggestions. Usually this means washing them in warm soapy water, then rinsing the lids and covering them with boiling water. Let the lids stay in the water until you are ready to use them.

PREPARING THE FRUIT

Before proceeding with any recipe, wash the fruit to remove any surface dust or pesticide residues. Wash fruit quickly in cold water. Do not allow the fruit to soak in the water, or vitamins will be leached out. Remove any stems or leaves, and hull the berries. Drain the fruit in colanders.

Be sure to cut away any bruises or bad spots. These rotting spots, if left, could lend an off-flavor to the preserve. As long as you are careful to remove any bad spots, less-than-perfect fruit can be used very successfully in preserves, particularly jams and jellies. Even overripe fruits can be used, but for best gelling results, use underripe or ripe fruits.

GETTING JAMS AND JELLIES TO GEL

There are two ways to make preserves gel—either you add pectin to the fruit, which causes it to gel, or you cook the fruits for as long a time as necessary, until the fruits gel. I prefer the long-cooking method.

Pectin is a naturally occurring substance in some fruits, and it makes the fruits gel. Apples are high in natural pectin, so apple preserves gel readily, without any added pectin. Peaches, berries, and grapes are low in natural pectin. You can buy several different types of commercial pectin to make your preserves gel. Most of these commercial pectins, such as Certo, are made from apples — so there is nothing unnatural or unhealthy about them.

The advantage of adding a commercial pectin to a preserve is that it enables you to make jams and jellies in a very short time. The preserves do not have to cook down a lot, so the volume is greater than with preserves that don't use commercial pectin.

The problem with most commerical pectins is that you must use a great deal of sugar to activate the pectin. The proportions are close to 1 part sugar to 1 part fruit. That's a lot of sugar! And I think you lose alot of fruit taste. Commercial pectins all come with their own recipes, so if you'd like to try making some jams or jellies that way, just buy a package or bottle of pectin.

You can also buy low-methoxyl pectin, which is designed to work with low-sugar recipes. This pectin is activated by calcium salts, which you buy along with the pectin. I've done some experimenting with low-methoxyl pectins, and I haven't been satisfied with the results. First, the jams were not flavorful enough because the pectin had to be dissolved in water, which dilutes the flavor. Second, the jams had a tendency to separate in the jars, so I had layers of jam and layers of runny liquid.

I haven't included any recipes for preserves using low-methoxyl pectin. However if you would like to experiment on your own, look for low-methoxyl pectin in your local supermarket, health food store, or food coop. There are several brands available and some come with recipes from the manufacturer. If you can't find any low-methoxyl pectin locally, write to Walnut Acres, Penns Creek, PA 17862.

Agar, a seaweed product, has been used with some success by some people to gel low-sugar jams. Again, I have not developed any recipes with agar that I've been satisfied with. You can find agar at most health food stores.

APPLES: FILLED WITH NATURAL PECTIN

Apples are filled with pectin. They can be added to any preserve to provide pectin for gelling. When I am extracting juice from such low-pectin fruits as ripe grapes, berries, peaches, apricots, pears, or cherries, I cut up about 4 apples (underripe ones are best) and throw them into the steamer with the other fruit. Or I peel and core a few apples and puree them in the food processor to add to low-pectin fruit purees when I am making jam. The flavor of the apples is not noticeable, but I can count on the apples to make the jam or jelly gel.

Steps for Making Jams, Preserves, and Conserves

If you've never done any preserving, be sure to read over the section on the basics of canning in chapter 2. Then start with these recipes. They are almost foolproof.

Low-sugar jams do not have to cook as long as jellies. They are cooked until a drop of jam dropped on a cold plate holds its shape rather then spreading and running. Deciding when a jam has cooked enough requires a little bit of judgment on your part. But, if a batch of your jam should fail to gel properly (if you remove it from the heat too soon), use it as a topping for ice cream, yogurt, or pancakes and turn your failure into a success. I guarantee it will taste just fine.

Preserves and conserves are similar to jams, but the fruit is prepared a little differently.

PREPARING THE FRUIT

To make a jam, you will peel your fruits if necessary, then crush or puree them. Preserves and conserves are made with peeled and chopped fruits.

I use my food processor for much of the preparation. A food processor fitted with a steel blade quickly purees berries; although with a little effort, you can get the same results by crushing the berries with a potato masher. The processor is at its most useful, I think, when put to work finely chopping peeled apples, peaches, pears, and apricots. If you fit the food processor with the steel blade and use the pulsing action, you can get finely chopped, not pureed, fruit which is what you need for preserves and conserves.

If you want to make a seedless berry or grape jam, press the prepared fruit through a food mill or sieve to eliminate the seeds.

COOKING JAMS, PRESERVES, AND CONSERVES

When there is no added pectin, cooking jams is a simple matter of combining all the ingredients and cooking until the jam thickens. Besides the fruit, there is a sweetener (honey, pure maple syrup, or sugar), lemon juice to activate the natural pectin in the fruit, and sometimes spices, such as cinnamon. Recipes specify sweetener amounts, but a little more or less can be added to taste. The recipes here have been developed to taste like fruit, not sugar.

Jams should be cooked over medium-high heat to maintain a good vigorous boil. Stir frequently to avoid scorching.

When the jam begins to thicken, test for doneness by dropping a spoonful of hot jam onto a cold plate. The jam will eventually hold its shape, with little running. It will thicken further as it cools.

With preserves and conserves, sugar or honey is often added to the fruit to get the juices flowing. With hard fruits, such as apples and pears, water and a sweetener, or fruit juice, may be added to the fruit. Usually lemon juice is added. Then the mixture is cooked until the syrup is thickened. Again, stir frequently to avoid scorching.

PROCESSING JAMS, PRESERVES, AND CONSERVES

When the jam, preserve, or conserve is done, remove it from the heat and skim off any foam that has accumulated on the top. To prevent floating fruit (once processed, the fruit has a tendency to rise to the top of the jar and the liquid settles to the bottom), let the mixture cool slightly, stirring frequently, for about 5 minutes, before ladling into the canning jars.

Ladle the hot fruit mixture into hot sterilized half-pint canning jars, leaving ½ inch head space. Seal. Process in a boiling water bath or steam canner for 5 minutes. Remove the jars from the canner and adjust the seals, if necessary—that is, if you are using a bail-wire jar. Let the jars cool undisturbed for 12 hours. Then test the seals. Store any jars that have not sealed in the refrigerator and use quickly.

If you have any questions about these canning procedures, refer to chapter 2 for more detailed instructions.

Making Fruit Butters

Fruit butters are made from fruit pulp, slowly cooked until the flavor is very concentrated and the texture is velvety smooth and thick.

PREPARING THE FRUIT
When making fruit butters, you can simply halve or quarter the fruit and cook with the skins on, or you can peel first. If you cook the fruit with the skins on, you will have to strain the fruit through a food mill once the fruit softens. When you cook hard fruits, such as apples and pears, add just enough water or fruit juice (an inch or so in the bottom of the pot) to prevent scorching.

COOKING FRUIT BUTTERS
Butters burn and scorch easily. They can be cooked slowly on top of the stove for several hours, while you watch carefully and stir frequently. Or you can spread the unsweetened fruit pulp in a roasting pan and bake it in the oven at 200° F. for up to 8 hours. In either case, the butter is done when it will hold the trace of a spoon that is drawn through it.

I much prefer to slowly bake my fruit butters, rather than cook them on top of the stove. There's no scorching of pots when you bake butters. You can leave the baking butter unattended; just check on it once every hour or so and give it a stir to prevent a skin from forming on the top.

If you find it hard to set aside the time to bake butters, do it in stages. I usually start baking in the evening, because the evening is when I have the time to cook and strain the fruit. I bake the butter until bedtime. Then I shut off the oven, and leave the butter inside. In the morning, I turn the oven back on and finish the baking.

The sweetener plays no role in thickening a fruit butter; it can be added to taste once the butter has thickened. This way the extra sweetener doesn't make it more likely that the butter will scorch. Also, the flavor of a fruit butter becomes more concentrated as it cooks down. Waiting until the end of the cooking or baking process to add the sweetener guarantees that the flavor will be just right for you—not too sweet and not too tart.

PROCESSING FRUIT BUTTERS

Ladle the hot butter into sterilized half-pint canning jars, leaving ¼ inch head space. Tap the bottom of the jar sharply against the counter to force out any air bubbles. Seal. Process in a boiling water bath or steam canner for 5 minutes. Adjust seals, if necessary. Let cool undisturbed for 12 hours. Check for a good seal. Store in a cool, dark place. (For more details on how to process, see chapter 2.)

• JAM RECIPES •

STRAWBERRY JAM WITH APPLES

Strawberries are low in pectin, so you must add some pectin if you want the jam to gel. I've tried low-methoxyl pectin, and the jam tended to separate. I've used agar, and again the jam separated. I've used commercial liquid pectin and couldn't taste the strawberries for the sugar.

In this recipe, the apples add pectin, but no discernable apple flavor. They do add a slight crunchiness to the texture, but I find that pleasing.

Peel, core, and chop the apples *very* finely. I do this in the food processor.

In a large nonaluminum pot, crush the prepared strawberries. A potato masher does this job easily. Add the honey and lemon juice. Bring to a boil and simmer until thick, 20–30 minutes. The jam is ready when it holds its shape when dropped onto a cold plate.

Remove from the heat. Skim off any foam that collects on the surface. Ladle the hot jam into hot sterilized half-pint jars, leaving ½ inch head space. Seal. Process in a boiling water bath or steam canner for 5 minutes. Adjust seals if necessary. Store in a cool, dry place. Once opened, store in the refrigerator. Strawberry jam seems to be more prone to mold than other fruit jams, so use it up quickly.

4	tart apples
12	cups fresh or frozen strawberries
1⅓	cups honey or sugar
¼	cup lemon juice

YIELD: **About 12 half-pints**

STRAWBERRY RHUBARB JAM

8   cups fresh or frozen
     strawberries
8   cups fresh or frozen
     rhubarb, cut in ½ inch
     pieces
4   cups honey or sugar
2   tablespoons lemon juice
2   teaspoons cinnamon

YIELD: **About 10 half-pints**

Frozen berries from last season in the freezer and another harvest season coming on? Make Strawberry Rhubarb Jam with fresh or frozen berries and fresh or frozen rhubarb.

If the strawberries are fresh, put them in a large kettle and crush them with a potato masher. Add the rhubarb and remaining ingredients. If the berries are frozen, combine them with the other ingredients in a large kettle. They should fall apart as they cook.

Bring the mixture to a boil and continue to boil, stirring frequently, until the mixture thickens, about 40 minutes. The jam is ready when it begins to hold its shape when dropped onto a cold plate.

Remove the jam from the heat. Skim off any foam. Ladle the hot jam into hot, sterilized half-pint jars, leaving ½ inch head space. Seal. Process in a boiling water bath or steam canner for 5 minutes. Adjust seals if necessary. Cool undisturbed for 12 hours. Store in a cool, dry place. Keep opened jars in the refrigerator.

BLUEBERRY JAM

Process half the blueberries in a food processor until mostly pureed, but still somewhat chunky. Or, place half the blueberries in a kettle and crush with a potato masher. This will take some effort.

Then, combine all the ingredients in a large kettle. Bring to a boil and boil vigorously until the mixture is fairly thick, about 30 minutes. You have reached the jam stage when a spoonful of jam dropped onto a cold plate begins to hold its shape.

Remove from the heat. Skim off any foam. Ladle the hot jam into hot, sterilized half-pint jars, leaving ½ inch head space. Seal. Process in a boiling water bath or steam canner for 5 minutes. Adjust seals, if necessary. Cool jars undisturbed for 12 hours. Store in a cool, dry place. Store opened jars in the refrigerator.

8	cups fresh or frozen blueberries
3	tablespoons lemon juice
1	cup sugar or honey
½	teaspoon cinnamon

YIELD: **5 half-pints**

MANY BERRY JAM

4   quarts fresh or frozen raspberries, blackberries, strawberries (any combination of quantities)
3   tart apples, finely chopped
1   cup honey
2   tablespoons lemon juice

YIELD: **8 half-pints**

This is one of my favorite jams. By combining the berries, I seem to get more flavor — the best of each berry. Many Berry Jam can be made with fresh or frozen berries. With frozen berries, it seems that the raspberries and blackberries break down more than the strawberries. The result is like a strawberry preserve in a raspberry jam. Delicious!

Crush a layer of berries in the bottom of a large kettle. Add the remaining berries and the rest of the ingredients. Bring to a boil and boil vigorously until the jam thickens, about 30 minutes. Stir frequently. The jam is ready when it begins to hold its shape when dropped onto a cold plate.

Remove from the heat at once. Skim off any foam. Ladle the hot jam into hot, sterilized half-pint jars, leaving ½ inch head space. Seal. Process in a boiling water bath or steam canner for 5 minutes. Adjust seals if necessary. Let cool undisturbed for 12 hours. Store in a cool, dry place. Store opened jars in the refrigerator.

BLACKBERRY JAM WITH APPLES

Wild blackberries tend to vary widely in degree of ripeness and sweetness. More sweetener can be added to taste.

Peel, core, and very finely chop the apples. I do this in a food processor.

In a large nonaluminum pot, crush half the berries. Add the remaining berries, apples, lemon juice, and cinnamon. Add the honey. Bring to a boil and boil gently for about 10 minutes, until thick. The jam is ready when it begins to hold its shape when dropped onto a cold plate.

Remove from the heat and skim off any foam. Ladle the hot jam into hot, sterilized half-pint jars, leaving ½ inch head space. Seal. Process in a boiling water bath or steam canner for 5 minutes. Adjust the seals if necessary. Store in a cool, dry place. Keep opened jars in the refrigerator.

4   tart apples
14 cups fresh or frozen blackberries (or black raspberries)
1   tablespoon lemon juice
1   teaspoon cinnamon
Approximately 2 cups honey (more to taste)

YIELD: **About 14 half-pints**

MAPLE PEACH JAM

5   pounds peaches
¼   cup lemon juice
1   cup pure maple syrup or honey
1   teaspoon cinnamon

YIELD: **About 10 half-pints**

Blanch the peaches in boiling water to cover for 1 minute to loosen the skins. Drain, cool, and peel. Remove the pits and chop very finely. I use a food processor to chop the peaches.

In a large nonaluminum pot, combine the peaches, lemon juice, maple syrup, and cinnamon. Bring to a boil and gently boil for about 10 minutes, until thick. The jam is ready when it begins to hold its shape when dropped onto a cold plate.

Remove from the heat. Skim off any foam that appears on the surface. Ladle the hot jam into hot, sterilized half-pint jars, leaving ½ inch head space. Seal. Process in a boiling water bath or steam canner for 5 minutes. Adjust seals if necessary. Store in a cool, dry place. Store opened jars in the refrigerator.

SWEET CHERRY JAM

Cherries contain plenty of pectin, so you don't have to worry about gelling with this fruit. Even though the proportion of fruit to sweetener in this jam is 8 to 1, the jam may be too sweet for some. Since sugar is a preservative, it is better to add more lemon juice to cut the sweetness.

Puree the fruit in a food processor or blender. In a large saucepan, combine the cherries, lemon juice, and sugar. Bring to a boil and boil until the jam begins to thicken, 10–15 minutes. The jam is ready when a spoonful dropped onto a cold plate begins to hold its shape.

Remove from the heat. Skim off any foam. Ladle the hot jam into hot, sterilized half-pint jars, leaving ½ inch head space. Seal. Process in a boiling water bath or steam canner for 5 minutes. Adjust seals if necessary. Let cool undisturbed for 12 hours. Store in a cool, dry place. Store opened jars in the refrigerator.

8   cups pitted sweet cherries
2   tablespoons lemon juice
1   cup sugar or honey

YIELD: **8 half-pints**

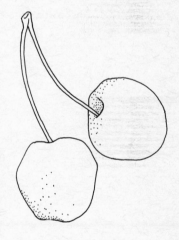
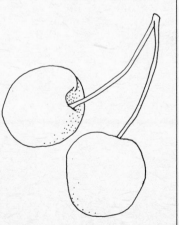

APPLE GRAPE JAM

8 cups peeled chopped apples
½ cup water
½ cup lemon juice
12 cups fresh Concord grape juice (page 138)
4 cups honey
4 teaspoons cinnamon

YIELD: **About 10 half-pints**

I can't decide which way I prefer this jam: with the cinnamon or without. The cinnamon adds a special spicy touch; but without it, the flavors of the apples and grapes remain distinct. If you like, ladle half the jam without cinnamon into the jars, then add 2 teaspoons of cinnamon into the remaining jam.

In a large kettle, combine the apples, water, and lemon juice. Cook until the apples are soft, about 10 minutes. Add the honey, grape juice, and cinnamon.

Bring to a boil, and boil rapidly, stirring frequently, until the mixture becomes quite thick. The jam is ready when it begins to hold its shape when dropped onto a cold plate.

Remove from the heat and skim off any foam. Ladle into hot, sterilized half-pint jars, leaving ½ inch head space. Seal. Process in a boiling water bath for 5 minutes. Adjust seals if necessary. Let cool undisturbed for 12 hours. Store in a cool, dry place. Store opened jars in the refrigerator.

MAPLE APPLE JAM

Tastes like apple pie in a jar . . .

A food processor does the best job of finely chopping apples in the least amount of time.

Combine all the ingredients in a large kettle. Bring to a boil, and continue to boil until the mixture thickens, about 10 minutes. The jam is ready when it begins to hold its shape when dropped onto a cold plate.

Remove from the heat and skim off any foam. Ladle into hot, sterilized half-pint jars, leaving ½ inch head space. Seal. Process in a boiling water bath or steam canner for 5 minutes. Adjust seals if necessary. Cool undisturbed for 12 hours. Store in a cool, dry place. Store opened jars in the refrigerator.

16 cups peeled finely chopped apples
1½ cups pure maple syrup
2 cups cider
1 teaspoon cinnamon
1 tablespoon lemon juice

YIELD: **About 12 half-pints**

APPLE BLUEBERRY PRESERVES

16 cups peeled finely chopped apples

2 cups cranberry juice

1 tablespoon lemon juice

2 cups honey or sugar

1 teaspoon grated lemon peel

4 cups fresh or frozen blueberries

YIELD: About 12 half-pints

When these preserves first go into the jar, it looks like apple sauce with the blueberries stirred in. As the jars sit on the shelf, the blueberries slowly stain the apple mixture a rich rosy purple.

The food processor does an excellent job of chopping the apples. If you are chopping by hand, you can dice the apples, then cook them with the cranberry juice until they are quite soft, about 5 minutes. Then, mash the apples with a potato masher for a nice, even consistency.

Otherwise, combine the chopped apples, cranberry juice, lemon juice, honey, and lemon peel in a large kettle. Cook until the mixture has thickened, about 15 minutes.

Remove from the heat. Skim off any foam. Gently fold in the berries. Stir as little as possible to evenly distribute the berries. Ladle the hot jam into clean, hot half-pint jars, leaving ½ inch head space. Seal. Process in a boiling water bath or steam canner for 10 minutes. Adjust seals if necessary. Let cool undisturbed for 12 hours. Store in a cool, dry place. Keep opened jars in the refrigerator.

SWEET CHERRY PRESERVES

These preserves will give you large cherry pieces floating in a not-too-sweet syrup—delicious on pancakes, waffles, and ice cream.

Puree 1 cup of the cherries in a food processor or blender. In a large saucepan, combine the pureed fruit, honey, lemon juice, and cinnamon. Bring to a boil and boil until the syrup reaches the jelly point at 220° F.

Remove from the heat. Skim off any foam. Stir in the rest of the fruit. Let stand for 5 minutes, stirring occasionally to prevent floating fruit. Ladle the hot preserves into clean, hot half-pint jars, leaving ½ inch head space. Seal. Process in a boiling water bath or steam canner for 10 minutes. Adjust seals if necessary. Let cool undisturbed for 12 hours. Store in a cool, dry place.

6 cups pitted fresh sweet cherries
1½ cups honey or sugar
2 tablespoons lemon juice
½ teaspoon cinnamon

YIELD: **5 half-pints**

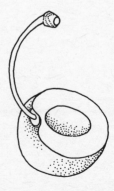

HONEYDEW LIME PRESERVES

7–8 cups diced honeydew (1 honeydew melon)

1½ cups sugar

2 apples

½ inch piece ginger root

Juice of 1 lime

YIELD: **3 pints**

These preserves make a wonderful topping for vanilla ice cream—and they are very simple to make.

Combine the honeydew and sugar in a large nonaluminum kettle. Let stand until a syrup forms, about 15 minutes.

Meanwhile, peel and quarter the apple. Peel the ginger, and mince both very finely in a food processor. Stir into the honeydew along with the lime juice. Bring to a boil and boil for about 10 minutes, until the sauce thickens.

Remove from the heat and let stand for 5 minutes to prevent floating fruit. Stir occasionally. Pack into clean, hot pint jars, leaving ½ inch head space. Seal. Process in a boiling water bath or steam canner for 10 minutes. Adjust seals if necessary. Let cool undisturbed for 12 hours. Store in a cool, dry place.

MINTED PEAR PRESERVES

A delicious, elegant topping for vanilla ice cream. Add some blueberries and you have a wonderful compote.

Choose a firm-fleshed pear, such as Seckel or Kieffer.

Peel, quarter, core, and thinly slice the pears. You should have about 6 cups. As you slice the pears, drop them into the cider in a large non-aluminum saucepan. This will prevent the pears from browning.

Add the mint leaves and honey to the saucepan. Bring to a boil and boil for 10 minutes. Remove from the heat and skim off any foam. Remove the mint leaves. Let stand for 5 minutes to prevent floating fruit in the jars. Stir occasionally.

Place a fresh sprig of mint in each clean, hot half-pint jar. Ladle the pears and syrup into the jars, leaving ½ inch head space. Seal. Process in a boiling water bath or steam canner for 10 minutes. Adjust seals if necessary. Let cool undisturbed for 12 hours. Store in a cool, dry place. Store opened jars in the refrigerator.

2½ pounds firm, slightly underripe pears

2 cups fresh cider or unpasteurized apple juice

10 fresh mint leaves

¼ cup honey (or more to taste)

6 sprigs fresh mint

YIELD: **About 6 half-pints**

BLUEBERRY PEACH CONSERVE

4   peaches
4   cups blueberries
1   orange (juice and rind)
½   cup honey or sugar
1   cup chopped walnuts

YIELD: **7 half-pints**

Peel the peaches by first immersing in boiling water for 1 minute. This should loosen the skins. Cool the peaches and slip off the skins. Pit and chop finely. You can use the food processor fitted with a steel blade to chop the peaches. Use the pulsing action and do not overprocess.

Puree half the blueberries in the food processor. Or, place half the blueberries in a large kettle and mash the berries with a potato masher. This will take some effort if the berries are firm, cultivated berries.

Very thinly peel the orange to remove the rind only. Avoid the white membrane. Finely chop the rind. Again, this is easy to do in a food processor. Squeeze the juice from the orange.

In a large kettle, combine the blueberries, peaches, orange juice and rind, honey, and walnuts. Bring to a boil and boil for 20–35 minutes until the mixture is thick and the fruits are tender.

Remove from the heat. Ladle the hot conserve into clean, hot half-pint jars, leaving ½ inch head space. Seal. Process in a boiling water bath or steam canner for 10 minutes. Adjust seals if necessary. Cool undisturbed for 12 hours. Store in a cool, dry place. Store opened jars in the refrigerator.

GRAPE CONSERVE

In a large covered kettle, combine the grapes and water. Cook until the grapes are quite soft, about 10 minutes. Strain through a food mill to remove the seeds and skins. You will have about 4 cups of grape puree.

In a nonaluminum saucepan, combine the grape puree, pear, lemon, honey, and cinnamon. Bring to a boil over medium high heat and boil for about 15 minutes. Add the nuts and continue to boil until the mixture becomes thick, 10–15 minutes more. The conserve should have jam-like consistency.

Remove from the heat. Ladle the hot conserve into clean, hot half-pint jars, leaving ½ inch head space. Seal. Process in a boiling water bath or steam canner for 10 minutes. Adjust seals if necessary. Let cool undisturbed for 12 hours. Store in a cool, dry place. Keep opened jars in the refrigerator.

8	cups Concord grapes (no stems)
½	cup water
1	pear, peeled and finely chopped
½	lemon, finely chopped
1 ½ –2	cups honey or sugar
1	tablespoon cinnamon
1	cup chopped almonds or walnuts

YIELD: **About 5 half-pints**

PEAR BUTTER

6 cups peeled sliced pears
2 cups water
1 tablespoon lemon juice
1 inch cube fresh ginger root
1 tablespoon pure maple syrup or honey or more to taste (optional)
¼ teaspoon ground allspice
3 cinnamon sticks (optional)

YIELD: 3 half-pints

The sweetener in this recipe is totally optional. Depending on which variety of pear you use, you may not want to add any additional sweetening to this concentrated butter. Bartlett pears are particularly sweet and easy to use.

As you peel, slice, and measure the pears, combine them with the water and lemon juice in a nonaluminum saucepan. I use an enamel-coated saucepan for making butters and have little trouble with scorching.

Bring the pears, water, and lemon juice to a boil. Cook until the pears are fairly soft, 5–10 minutes.

Peel the ginger root. Cut into quarters and place in a food processor fitted with a steel blade. Finely mince the ginger. Add the pears and puree together. You will probably have to do this step in 2 batches.

Return the pureed pears to the kettle or saucepan and cook over low heat for about 2 hours until the pear butter is very thick. The butter will cook down considerably; when you draw a spoon through the mixture, you should be able to see the path that the spoon makes through the butter. As the pears cook down, stir frequently to avoid scorching.

When the butter is sufficiently thick, remove from the heat. Taste. If desired, stir in the sweetener. Stir in the allspice.

Place a cinnamon stick in each hot, sterilized half-pint canning jar. Ladle in the hot butter, leaving ¼ inch head space. Seal. Process in a boiling water bath or steam canner for 5 minutes. Let cool undisturbed for 12 hours. Store in a cool, dry place. Keep opened jars in the refrigerator.

BAKED GRAPE BUTTER

With this method of baking the butter to thicken it, there are no scorched pots to worry about. And the flavor is deliciously densely grape.

Combine the grapes and water in a large kettle. Cover and steam until the grapes are very soft, 10–15 minutes. Stir occasionally.

Strain the grapes through a food mill to remove the seeds and skins. You will be left with 9–10 cups of thick grape juice. Pour the thick grape juice into a roasting pan. Set the pan in the oven and bake at 200° F. until the butter is quite thick, 5–8 hours. Stir occasionally, at least once an hour, to prevent a skin from forming.

You can begin baking at night, turn the oven off before you go to bed, and resume baking in the morning. The baking time will depend on the size of your pan, whether it has been left in a warm oven overnight, and how thick a butter you want. The butter is done when it has reached a desirable thick consistency. I call the butter done when it will hold a trace of a spoon stirring the mixture.

When the butter is thick, remove it from the oven. You will have 3–4 cups of concentrated, tart grape butter. Sweeten to taste with honey or sugar. Add cinnamon to taste. Return the butter to the top of the stove or the oven to reheat.

Ladle the hot butter into hot, sterilized half-pint jars, leaving ¼ inch head space. Seal. Process in a boiling water bath or steam canner for 5 minutes. Adjust seals if necessary. Let cool undisturbed for 12 hours. Store in a cool, dry place. Store opened jars in the refrigerator.

4   quarts Concord grapes (no stems, about 4 pounds)
¼   cup water
¾ –1 cup honey or sugar
     About 2 teaspoons cinnamon (optional)

YIELD: 4–5 half-pints

BAKED APPLE BUTTER

10 pounds apples (about 20 apples)

1 cup water

Pure maple syrup, honey, or molasses (optional)

Cinnamon (optional)

Nutmeg (optional)

YIELD: 4–5 half-pints

This is the no-fuss, no scorch way to make apple butter. By the way, you can use any variety of apple to make fruit butters—including unbruised drops.

Quarter the apples and combine with the water in a large covered kettle. Bring the water to a boil and steam the apples until they are quite soft, 20–30 minutes. Let the apples cool slightly.

Strain the apples through a food mill. You will have about 10 cups of pink apple puree. Pour the apple puree into a large roasting pan. Place the puree in the oven, turn the heat to 200° F., and slowly bake the apple butter until it is quite thick, 6–8 hours. Stir occasionally, at least once an hour, to prevent a skin from forming.

You can, if you like, interrupt the baking. Simply turn off the oven and leave the butter in the warmed oven, until you are ready to resume baking—within the day, that is.

The longer you bake the butter, the darker and thicker it will become. I bake my apple butter until it will hold the trace of a spoon when stirred. Many people like to cook down apple butter until it has the spreading consistency of a soft peanut butter. Your baking time will depend on the size of your roasting pan, whether you interrupt the baking or not, and how thick you want the butter to be.

When the butter has reached the desired thickness, remove it from the oven. Stir in the sweetener and spices. Taste as you go. Return the butter to the oven or the top of the stove to reheat for canning.

Ladle the hot butter into hot, sterilized half-pint jars, leaving ¼ inch head space. Seal. Process in boiling water bath or steam canner for 5 minutes. Adjust seals if necessary. Let cool undisturbed for 12 hours. Store in a cool, dry place. Keep opened jars in the refrigerator.

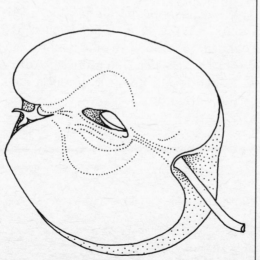
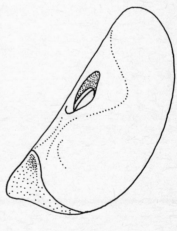

FRUGAL APPLE BUTTER

10   **pounds apples, peeled, cored, and quartered**

½   **cup pure maple syrup, honey, or sugar (more to taste)**

½   **teaspoon cinnamon (more to taste)**

YIELD: **6 half-pints**

This is the apple butter to make if you have a steam juicer. First you extract all the juice for jelly. Then you cook down the remaining apple pulp into apple butter. The apples are peeled before they are steamed to create a light colored butter. However, if you prefer, don't peel the apples. Before combining the apples with the syrup and cinnamon, strain through a food mill.

Steam the apples to extract the juice. You will be left with about 4 cups of juice and 8 cups of apple pulp. Drink the juice or use it in jelly.

Combine the apple pulp with the syrup and cinnamon in a heavy saucepan. Simmer over low heat for 3–4 hours, until the mixture is so thick it holds it shape and will form peaks like beaten egg whites. Stir occasionally to prevent scorching.

When the apple butter has thickened, ladle into hot, sterilized half-pint jars, leaving ¼ inch head space. Run a chopstick along the inside of the jar to remove any air bubbles. Seal. Process in a boiling water bath or steam canner for 5 minutes. Adjust seals if necessary. Let cool undisturbed for 12 hours. Store in a cool, dry place. Store opened jars in the refrigerator.

· 8 ·

Making Jellies & Marmalades

I love to see rows of sparkling clear jellies lining my cupboard shelves. The jellies are the most beautiful of all the preserves, I think. And I take special pride in the low-sugar jellies I make because they taste as good as they look.

Low-sugar jellies and marmalades taste like fruit. Many of these jellies and all the marmalades are appealingly tart, a perfect complement to a richly textured piece of homemade whole wheat bread.

Making jellies and marmalades is quite similar to making jams, preserves, and conserves. Jellies are made with fruit juice and marmalades are made of fruit juice and pieces of citrus fruit.

Making jellies and marmalades without adding lots of sugar and commercial pectin is a little tricky—even trickier than making jam. You have to work in small batches and watch carefully for the jelly stage (I *always* use a jelly thermometer). Sometimes you might even have failures—if you are using overripe low-pectin fruits, for example. There's a way to avoid that failure, however. When in doubt that you have sufficient pectin, throw a couple of apples in with the fruit when

Steam Juicer

Lid

Steamer

Juice Kettle

Drain Tube

Water Kettle

you are extracting the juice. The apple juice won't add flavor to the rest of the fruit juice, but it will contribute enough pectin to make the jelly gel.

What is pectin? It's a naturally occuring substance in many fruits, and it is what allows jelly to gel. If you are new to the art of making fruit preserves, I suggest that you read chapter 7 on making jams, preserves, conserves, and fruit butters before proceeding with making jellies. There are some valuable explanations of pectin and how to make jams and jellies gel.

The recipes in this chapter are all low-sugar recipes. Your jellies and marmalades made with these recipes will not keep as well as the high-sugar commercial products. To guarantee as long a shelf life as possible, put these up in sterilized half-pint jars and store opened jars in the refrigerator. Opened jars of jellies and marmalades can be expected to keep without fermenting or molding for about 3 months in the refrigerator. Perhaps they will keep longer, but they don't last that long in my house.

Making Jellies

Making jelly involves 2 steps: extracting the juice and then gelling the juice.

EXTRACTING FRUIT JUICE

The easiest way to extract juice is with a steam juicer. Steam juicers consist of 3 parts. On the bottom level is a pot that holds about 3 quarts of water. On top sits a pot into which the fruit juice is collected. On top of that is a steamer to hold the fruit. To assemble the juicer on the stove, fill the bottom well with water, and the top steamer with fruit. Place the cover on the steamer pot. Attach a clamped hose to the spout on the middle pot.

Usually you will steam the fruit for about 2 hours to extract all the juice. Then the juice is drained out of the collecting pot via the hose. It's very simple and there is little mess or clean-up involved.

With a steamer, there are 2 things to look out for. First, check the steamer every once in a while to be sure you don't run out of steaming water. And second, be sure the hose is securely clamped so that juice doesn't leak out.

Jelly Bags

If you don't have a steamer, you can cook your fruit in a little water to extract the juice. Hard fruits, such as apples, should be chopped or crushed. (Again, the food processor is handy here.) Place the fruit in a large kettle and add just enough water to prevent scorching. Then simmer the fruit until you have a juicy, pulpy mass.

To extract the juice, strain it through a *damp* jelly bag or several layers of *damp* cheesecloth. If you are using cheesecloth, it is easiest to line a colander with the cheesecloth and set the colander over a large bowl to collect the clear fruit juices. A jelly bag can be hung from a hook over a counter, and the juices collected in a bowl set beneath the bag. Don't yield to the temptation of squeezing the jelly bag to make the juice run faster. This will result in cloudy juice.

Be sure to thoroughly rinse your jelly bag or cheesecloth each time you use it. Rinse it in several changes of hot water.

A simpler way still to collect the pure fruit juice is to refrigerate the juicy pulp overnight in a tall container. The pulp and sediments will sink to the bottom of the container. In the morning, pour off the clear juice from the top of the container and discard the sediment on the bottom.

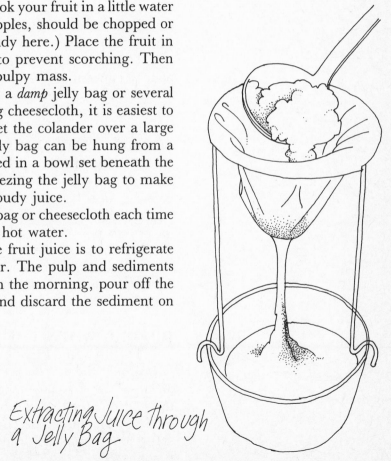

Extracting Juice through a Jelly Bag

CANNING OR FREEZING FRUIT JUICES

Fresh fruit juice can be used immediately or canned or frozen to be made into jelly later. To can the juice, heat it to simmering and pour into clean, hot quart jars, leaving ½ inch head space. Seal. Process in a boiling water bath or steam canner for 10 minutes. Adjust seals if necessary. Let cool undisturbed for 12 hours. Check for good seals (see chapter 2). Juice should be stored in a cool, dark place. Exposure to light may cause color and vitamin losses.

To freeze fresh fruit juice, first cool it to room temperature. Then pour the juice into freezer containers, leaving ½ inch head space and freeze. Defrost and stir well before using. If you want a more concentrated juice, pour off the clear liquid that rises to the top.

COOKING THE JUICE TO MAKE JELLY

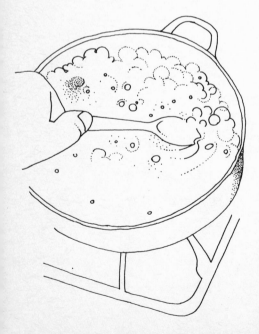

When you make jelly, you have to work in small batches—no more than 8 cups of fruit juice at a time. Don't be tempted to double your batches, because then it will take *hours* to reach the jelly stage. Meanwhile, you will run a good risk of having your jelly boil over the top of your pot. Worse still, overcooking can destroy the natural pectin in the fruit, guaranteeing that the fruit will never gel.

Select a large kettle. Combine the fruit juice and sugar. Bring the juice to a vigorous boil, stirring almost constantly. Keep the mixture boiling until the jelly stage is reached, 220° F. on a jelly themometer.

JUDGING WHEN THE JELLY STAGE IS REACHED

The first time I made jelly without added pectin, I was struck by how similar the process is to making maple syrup. At the sugar house, an experienced sugar-maker judges the readiness of the syrup, not by the hydrometer that the books recommend, but by the look of the bubbles. The large open bubbles of sap that has been boiled down to syrup look remarkably similar to fruit juice that has boiled down to become jelly.

When you are making jelly it seems to take forever to cook the fruit juice down to the jelly stage—particularly when you are making a low-sugar jelly. It is easy to fool yourself into thinking that your thermometer is faulty. Watch the bubbles. They will tell you whether or not you have reached the jelly stage.

When the ingredients first come to a boil, you can stir down the boil. Then the jelly begins a rolling boil. Bubbles appear as tiny pinpricks on the surface of the jelly. Then large, open bubbles begin to appear on the sides of the kettle.

When the volume has been reduced by about half, you get a very active boil. The surface becomes partially covered with rolling large, open bubbles. The temperature hovers around 215–218°F.

The bubbles get larger and larger, covering the surface of the jelly and beginning to climb up the sides of the kettle. At last, the surface of the jelly is solid with large, open bubbles. The jelly actively climbs up the sides of the kettle, and the temperature reaches 220°F. (or 8° above the temperature at which water boils at your altitude).

This bubble test is, in my opinion, much easier to observe than seeing if the jelly "sheets" off a metal spoon. In this test, a cold metal spoon is dipped into the jelly, then lifted out. Before the jelly is done, it will drip off the spoon in 2 distinct drops. Once the jelly stage has been reached, the jelly will drip off the spoon in 1 large drip, or "sheet."

When Jelly Drips off a Spoon in a Single Sheet it is Done

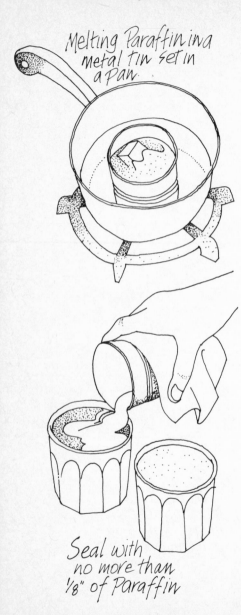

Melting Paraffin in a metal Tin set in a Pan

Seal with no more than 1/8" of Paraffin

You can also test by dropping some jelly onto a plate and putting the plate in the freezer for about 5 minutes. If the jelly is gelled after 5 minutes, then it is done. The problem with this test is that you have to remove the rest of the jelly from the heat during the test so you don't run the risk of overcooking your jelly. If you have to put the jelly back on the stove, you've wasted 5 minutes and will have to cook the jelly extra just to get it back to a boil.

If you should remove the jelly from the heat before the jelly stage has been reached, you won't notice your mistake until after the jelly has been sealed in jars and cooled. Then you will see that the jelly didn't gel. At this point, you can call it "syrup" and serve it on ice cream or pancakes, or you can empty the jars into the kettle and cook again until the jelly stage is reached.

SEALING THE JELLY

Jellies can be sealed with paraffin, they can be sealed by the open kettle canning method, or they can be processed. Since I've already heated my canner to sterilize my jars, I usually process my jellies for the added assurance of safety. But it is not necessary.

With Paraffin

You can find paraffin at the supermarket. It comes in solid blocks and must be melted before it can be used. Begin melting the paraffin before the jelly is ready. An easy way to do this is to place the paraffin in a clean metal coffee tin, place the tin in a pot of hot water, and melt the paraffin slowly over *low* heat. Any paraffin that is not used can be left in the tin, covered, and used at a later date.

Pour the hot jelly into hot, sterilized half-pint jars, leaving ¼ inch head space. Immediately pour a ⅛ inch layer of paraffin over the top of the jelly. Use a sterilized needle to prick any air bubbles that appear on the top of the paraffin. Don't pour more than ⅛ inch of paraffin on the jelly or it may fail to seal. Let the paraffin cool undisturbed. Then cover the jars with a plastic snap-on lid or a metal lid.

With Open Kettle Canning

Pour the hot jelly into hot, sterilized half-pint jars. Leave ⅛ inch head space. Seal with the 2-piece metal lid and screwband. Tighten the screwband. The jar should seal as the jelly cools. Test for seals after 12 hours (for details, see chapter 2). Any jars that have not sealed should be stored in the refrigerator and used quickly. Store sealed jars in a cool, dark place.

With Processing

Pour the hot jelly into hot, sterilized half-pint jars, leaving ⅛ inch head space. Seal. Process in a boiling water bath or steam canner for 5 minutes. Adjust seals, if necessary. Let cool undisturbed for 12 hours, then remove the screwbands and check for sealing. (See chapter 2 for details.) Store in a cool, dark place. Keep opened jars in the refrigerator.

Making Marmalades

Marmalades are cooked until the syrup reaches the jelly stage; in this they are like jellies. However, they are made up of fruit suspended in the jelly. In this they are like preserves. In the marmalade recipes which follow, the extra steps of boiling and cooling the fruit mixture prevent the citrus peels from toughening. Marmalades should be processed in a boiling water bath or steam canner for 5 minutes for safe keeping.

RASPBERRY JELLY

16 cups fresh raspberries
4 tart apples, chopped
2 cups sugar
2 tablespoons lemon juice

YIELD: **Approximately
4 half-pints**

Purple raspberries seem to retain their "raspberry" flavor better than red raspberries when they are canned, frozen, or made into jelly. Since raspberries are low in natural pectin, I cook a few apples with the raspberries to boost the pectin content, without affecting the taste.

Combine the raspberries and apples in a steam juicer and steam until all the juice is extracted from the berries, about 3 hours. You should have about 8 cups of juice.

Or, combine the berries and apples in a large kettle. Add about ¼ cup water to prevent the berries from scorching. Cook until the berries are thoroughly soft, about 10 minutes. Stir frequently. Remove from the heat and strain the berries and apples through a damp jelly bag. Do not squeeze the bag. Measure the juice into a large nonaluminum kettle. You should have about 8 cups of juice.

Add the sugar and lemon juice to the raspberry juice in the kettle. Bring to a boil and boil vigorously until the mixture reaches the jelly stage, 220° F.

Remove from the heat and skim off any foam. Ladle the hot jelly into hot, sterilized half-pint jars, leaving the proper amount of head space for the sealing method you choose. Seal according to the instructions on pages 142–143, using paraffin, open kettle canning, or processing. Cool undisturbed for 12 hours. Store in a cool, dry place. Store opened jars in the refrigerator.

CURRANT JELLY

Currants, like most fruit, have the most pectin when they are just ripe, or even, slightly underripe. So pick them young! Four quarts of currants will yield about 8 cups of juice.

Currants are quite tart. In this low-sugar recipe, I add just enough sugar to mellow the tartness. Add more to suit your taste, if you like.

Combine the currant juice and sugar in a large kettle. Bring to a boil and boil rapidly, stirring occasionally until the mixture reaches the jelly stage, 220° F., about 30 minutes. A thermometer is recommended.

Remove from the heat and skim off any foam. Ladle the hot jelly into hot, sterilized half-pint jars, leaving the proper amount of head space for the sealing method you choose. Seal according to the instructions on pages 142–143, using paraffin, open kettle canning, or processing. Cool undisturbed for 12 hours. Store in a cool, dry place. Store opened jars in the refrigerator.

8 cups currant juice
2 cups sugar (or more to taste)

YIELD: 4 half-pints

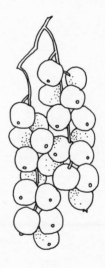

PLUM JELLY

8   **cups plum juice (about 5 pounds Italian prune plums)**

1½   **cups sugar or a little more to taste**

1   **tablespoon lemon juice**

½   **teaspoon cinnamon**

YIELD: **2–3 half-pints**

Combine the plum juice, sugar, lemon juice, and cinnamon. Stir to dissolve the sugar and taste. If you like, add more sugar. I like to make this jelly a little on the tart side. Bring to a boil and boil vigorously until the mixture reaches the jelly stage, 220° F. This will take about 1 hour.

Remove from the heat and skim off any foam. Ladle the hot jelly into hot, sterilized half-pint jars, leaving the proper amount of head space for the sealing method you choose. Seal according to the instructions on pages 142–143, using paraffin, open kettle canning, or processing. Cool undisturbed for 12 hours. Store in a cool, dry place. Store opened jars in the refrigerator.

GRAPE JELLY

Here's a low-sugar recipe that requires close to an hour of cooking to reach the jelly stage since grapes are very low in natural pectin. But you don't have to fuss over the jelly as it cooks. The end result: a nicely tart jelly that really tastes like grapes. If you like, throw in a couple of apples when you cook down the grapes to extract the juice.

Combine all the ingredients in a large kettle. Bring to a boil and boil rapidly, stirring occasionally, until the mixture reaches the jelly stage, 220° F., about 1 hour. A thermometer is recommended.

Remove from the heat and skim off any foam. Ladle the hot jelly into hot, sterilized half-pint jars, leaving the proper amount of head space for the sealing method you choose. Seal according to the instructions on pages 142–143, using paraffin, open kettle canning, or processing. Cool undisturbed for 12 hours. Store in a cool, dry place. Store opened jars in the refrigerator.

9	cups fresh Concord grape juice
3	cups sugar
¼	cup lemon juice

YIELD: 5–6 half-pints

APPLE JELLY

8 cups fresh apple juice
2 cups sugar
1 teaspoons cinnamon
1 tablespoons lemon juice

YIELD: 4 half-pints

Combine all the ingredients in a large kettle. Bring to a boil, and boil rapidly, stirring occasionally, until the mixture reaches the jelly stage, 220° F. A thermometer is recommended.

Remove from the heat and skim off any foam. Ladle the hot jelly into hot, sterilized half-pint jars, leaving the proper amount of head space for the sealing method you choose. Seal according to the instructions on pages 142–143, using paraffin, open kettle canning, or processing. Cool undisturbed for 12 hours. Store in a cool, dry place. Store opened jars in the refrigerator.

MINT APPLE JELLY

8 cups fresh apple juice
1½ cups sugar
1 cup fresh mint leaves
1 tablespoon lemon juice

YIELD: 3 half-pints

Combine the apple juice, sugar, mint leaves, and lemon juice in a heavy saucepan. Bring to a boil and boil just until the jelly reaches the gel point, 220° F. This will take about 1 hour.

Remove from the heat, skim off any foam and remove the mint leaves. Ladle the hot jelly into hot, sterilized half-pint jars, leaving the proper amount of head space for the sealing method you choose. Seal according to the instructions on pages 142–143, using paraffin, open kettle canning, or processing. Cool undisturbed for 12 hours. Store in a cool, dry place. Store opened jars in the refrigerator.

ELDERBERRY APPLE JELLY

The apple juice provides the pectin that the elderberry lacks and mellows the pungent flavor of the berries. Pick slightly underripe elderberries for jelly.

Combine the elderberry juice, apple juice, sugar, and lemon juice in a heavy saucepan. Bring to a boil and boil just until the jelly reaches the gel point, 220° F. This will take about 45 minutes.

Remove from the heat and skim off any foam. Ladle the hot jelly into hot, sterilized half-pint jars, leaving the proper amount of head space for the sealing method you choose. Seal according to the instructions on pages 142–143, using paraffin, open kettle canning, or processing. Cool undisturbed for 12 hours. Store in a cool, dry place. Store opened jars in the refrigerator.

8   **cups extracted elderberry juice**
4   **cups fresh unpasteurized apple juice**
1½   **cups sugar**
2   **tablespoons lemon juice**

YIELD: 2 half-pints

TROPICAL MARMALADE

1   grapefruit
4   oranges
2   lemons
    Approximately 10 cups
    water
    Approximately 4 cups
    honey or sugar

YIELD: **About 6 half-pints**

Scrub the fruit well. Peel the fruit, removing just the colored rind and leaving the bitter white pith. Reserve the rind, and peel away the white pith and discard. Finely chop the remaining fruit and rind. This is a laborious process by hand; use a food processor for best results.

Measure the fruit and juice. In a large nonaluminum pot, combine the fruit and juice with twice as much water. You should have about 5 cups of fruit and juice, to which you will add 10 cups of water. Bring to a boil, then simmer for 30 minutes. Remove from the heat and let stand for 12 hours.

Measure the fruit and juice again. You will have about 12 cups. For each cup of fruit and juice, add ⅓ cup honey or sugar. If you have 12 cups of fruit, add 4 cups of sweetener.

Bring the marmalade to a boil, and boil vigorously until the marmalade reaches the jelly stage, 200° F. This will take at least 30 minutes, depending on how vigorously the boil is maintained. As the marmalade reaches the jelly point, stir constantly to prevent scorching. When the jelly reaches 220° F., remove from the heat, and skim off any foam. If the marmalade should become extremely thick before you reach 220° F., remove from the heat when it reaches a good spreading thickness.

Ladle the hot marmalade into hot, sterilized half-pint jars, leaving ½ inch head space. Seal. Process in a boiling water bath or steam canner for 5 minutes. Adjust seals if necessary. Let cool undisturbed for 12 hours. Store in a cool, dry place. Store opened jars in the refrigerator.

LEMON LIMEALADE

This marmalade tastes as refreshing as lemonade. It is surprisingly delicious as an ice cream topping.

Scrub the fruit well. Peel the limes and lemons, removing just the colored rind and leaving the bitter white pith. Reserve the rind, and peel away the white pith and discard. Finely chop the remaining fruit and rind. This is a laborious process by hand; use a food processor for best results.

Measure the fruit and juice. In a large nonaluminum pot, combine the fruit and juice with twice as much water. You should have about 3 cups of fruit and juice, to which you will add 6 cups of water. Bring to a boil, then simmer for 30 minutes. Remove from the heat and let stand for 12 hours.

Measure the fruit and juice again. You will have about 6 cups. For each cup of fruit and juice, add ½ cup honey or sugar. If you have 6 cups of fruit, add 3 cups of sweetener.

Bring the marmalade to a boil, and boil vigorously until the marmalade reaches the jelly stage, 200° F. This will take at least 30 minutes, depending on how vigorously the boil is maintained. As the marmalade reaches the jelly point, stir constantly to prevent scorching. When the jelly reaches 220° F., remove from the heat, and skim off the foam.

Ladle the hot marmalade into hot, sterilized half-pint jars, leaving ½ inch head space. Seal. Process in a boiling water bath or steam canner for 5 minutes. Adjust seals if necessary. Let cool undisturbed for 12 hours. Store in a cool, dry place. Store opened jars in the refrigerator.

6   limes
2   lemons
    Approximately 6 cups water
    Approximately 3 cups honey or sugar

YIELD: **6–7 half-pints**

ORANGE PEAR MARMALADE

4   oranges
     Water
     Honey
2   pears, peeled and finely chopped
1   teaspoon powdered ginger

YIELD: **About 5 half-pints**

Scrub the oranges. Cut into quarters, seed, and finely chop — skins and all. I like to do this step in the food processor. Measure the fruit and orange juice and pour into a large nonaluminum kettle. You will have 3–4 cups. Combine with 2 times as much water. Let stand for 12 hours.

Bring the orange and juice mixture to a boil and simmer for 30 minutes. Let stand for 2 hours. Measure the fruit and juice. For every cup of this mixture, add ¼ cup honey. Add the pears and ginger. Bring to a boil and boil vigorously until the jelly stage, 220° F., is reached. This will take about 1 hour, depending on how vigorously the boil is maintained. Stir frequently. As the marmalade comes close to the jelly stage, stir constantly to prevent scorching. Skim off any foam that appears.

When the jelly stage is reached, ladle the hot marmalade into hot, sterilized half-pint jars, leaving ¼ inch head space. Seal. Process in a boiling water bath or steam canner for 5 minutes. Adjust seals if necessary. Let cool undisturbed for 12 hours. Store in a cool, dry place. Store opened jars in the refrigerator.

Appendix

Jams and Jellies:

WHAT WENT WRONG?

Preserves or Jellies are Too Soft. Preserves or jellies that are too soft probably did not cook long enough.

Use the jelly as syrup, or try again. Do not return more than 8 cups of jelly to the kettle at a time. Boil vigorously until the jelly registers 220° F. on your jelly thermometer. Ladle into hot, sterilized half-pint jars and seal.

If you doubled the recipe, which is never advised, the jelly could be too soft because it was cooked too long. Serve it as syrup.

Runny preserves and jams should probably be served as they are. They may be too soft because the storage area is too warm. If this is the problem, remove the jars to a cooler storage area.

Jelly or Jam Is Too Hard. A jelly or jam that is too hard was overcooked. There really isn't much you can do about it. It will still taste good.

"Weepy" Jelly. When you open a jar of jelly, you notice that there are beads of liquid on the top. Usually this indicates the jelly is stored at too warm a temperature. There is nothing wrong with this jelly, but other jars should be moved to a cooler place to prevent further deterioration. Sometimes too much acid will cause a jelly to weep.

Mold or Fermentation. This indicates that your jars did not seal properly, or that you did not use sterilized jars and lids. Throw it out; it can't be salvaged.

Fresh Fruit Yields

FRUIT	WEIGHT	QUANTITY	YIELD
Apples	1 pound	6 medium	3 cups, chopped
Apricots	1 pound	8–14 medium	2 cups, halved
Berries	1 pound	1 pint	2 cups
Cherries	1 pound	3 cups	2 cups, pitted
Currants	1 pound	2½ cups	
Grapefruit	1 pound	1 large	1¾ cups, chopped
Grapes	1 pound	2⅔ cups	2 cups, pitted
Oranges	1 pound	2 medium	1 cup, chopped
Peaches	1 pound	3–5 medium	2–2½ cups, chopped
Pears	1 pound	4–5 medium	2⅔ cups, chopped
Plums	1 pound	12–20 medium	2 cups, sliced
Rhubarb	1 pound	4–8 stalks	

Fresh Vegetable Yields

VEG.	WEIGHT	QUANTITY	YIELD
Beans, green	1 pound	3–4 cups	3 ⅔ cups, trimmed
Beets	1 pound	4–6 medium	3 ½ cups, cooked and sliced
Cabbage	2 pounds	1 medium head	7–8 cups, shredded
Carrots	1 pound	6 medium	2 ½ cups, sliced
Cauliflower	1 ½ pounds	1 medium head	4 cups florets
Celery	1 pound	8–12 stalks	4 cups, diced
Corn		8–10 ears	4 cups kernels
Cucumbers	1 pound	5 small	2 cups, sliced
Okra	1 pound		4 cups
Peppers	1 pound	4 large	2 cups, chopped
Tomatoes	1 pound	4 medium	3 cups, chopped
Zucchini	1 pound	3 medium	2 ¼ cups, sliced

Adjusting for Altitiude

If you live 1,000 feet or more above sea level, you must adjust your canning times accordingly. This will definitely affect the quality of your pickles, I am sorry to say. Pickles that are fermented in a crock and stored in a refrigerator are your best bet if you live more than 5,000 feet above sea level.

The quality of your preserves, jams, and jellies will not be affected by the increased canning times, but the point at which your jelly gels will be 8° above the temperature at which water boils, and not 220° F.

ALTITUDE (IN FEET)	INCREASE PROCESSING TIME BY:
1,000	1 minute
2,000	2 minutes
3,000	3 minutes
4,000	4 minutes
5,000	5 minutes
6,000	6 minutes
7,000	7 minutes
8,000	8 minutes
9,000	9 minutes
10,000	10 minutes

Index

Numbers in italics refer to illustrations.